THE ART DECO HOUSE

THE ART DECO HOUSE

Avant-Garde Houses of the 1920s and 1930s

ADRIAN TINNISWOOD

WATSON-GUPTILL PUBLICATIONS
NEW YORK

First published in the United States in 2002
by Watson-Guptill Publications, a division of
VNU Business Media, Inc., 770 Broadway,
New York, NY 10003
www.watsonguptill.com

Executive Editor **Mark Fletcher**
Executive Art Editor **Christie Cooper**
Project Editor **Emily Asquith**
Copy Editor **Richard Dawes**
Designer **John Round**
Picture Researcher **Jenny Faithfull**
Production **Alex Wiltshire**
Proof reader **Nicola Kearton**
Indexer **Sue Farr**

Half title page: Leaflet design for the 1925 Paris
Exposition; Title page: Mirror by Eileen Gray, Villa
Turque, La Chaux-de-Fonds, Switzerland; Right: Detail
of a door panel, 375 Madison Avenue, New York

ISBN 0-8230-0315-9

Library of Congress Control Number: 2001095177

Set in Sabon and Quadraat Sans

Printed and bound in China

CONTENTS

BRAVE NEW WORLDS

One of the big issues that exercised the minds and consciences of architects and social commentators between the two world wars was the future of domestic architecture. What form should the house take in order to meet the requirements of modern life?

This preoccupation with the house as a genre was a hangover from the days of the Arts and Crafts movement, whose members held the home to be the most important prerequisite for a happy and fulfilled life, and who therefore focused on the design of houses to the exclusion of almost every other form of architecture. It is no coincidence that, well into the twentieth century, the British name for the Arts and Crafts movement was "the Domestic Revival."

To the Brave New World of the 1920s, the domestic values that William Morris and his followers had emphasized so strongly – stability, continuity, tranquillity, and tradition – didn't seem quite so appropriate in a society that, instead of turning its back on industrialization, had grown to depend on its benefits and to look forward with bated breath to the next technological advance. Some architects, it is true, thought that the historicist vocabulary that had stood them in good stead for decades was in no need of alteration; and

RIGHT Elegant, opulent, and indomitably conservative, this salon, designed in 1925 by the teacher, writer, and *ensemblier* André Fréchet, epitomizes French Art Deco at its peak.

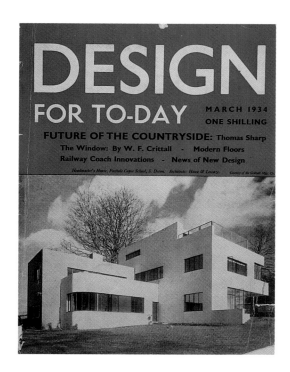

on both sides of the Atlantic neo-Georgian mansions and quaint, rambling "cottages" with inglenook fireplaces continued to appear in alarming numbers. The only concession such architects made to modernity was to provide equally quaint half-timbered outbuildings to hide their clients' cars and electricity generators. But others were equally certain that domestic architecture in the post-war world needed a radical change of direction. How could it contribute to the technological utopia promised by the pundits, a Hollywood heaven of luxurious, labor-saving living and mass car ownership?

One route was to develop a design vocabulary that jettisoned the cultural baggage of the past, in favor of the technology that promised so much. The car, great symbol of a liberated future, was held up as a shining example: Le Corbusier praised it in the 1920s; and, bewailing the state of contemporary British design a decade later, the British architect Robert Gardner-Medwin wrote that "there is still a prejudice against furniture which is mass-produced, even among people who enjoy driving in a mass-produced car... If the furniture industry were as competitive and as competently organized as the motor industry … it would be possible for families of all incomes to buy soundly constructed, elegantly appropriate furniture."

But it was not only the methods of the manufacturing industry that were appealing. There was also the look: the dynamic qualities that references to the machine could impart to something as intrinsically static as a house, making it seem as though it were rushing headlong to meet the future, rather than gazing longingly over its shoulder at the past.

At the end of the 1930s, Patrick Abercrombie, Professor of Town Planning at London University, summed up trends in residential architecture in a slightly bemused and wholly British way. As well as marveling at "momentary aberrations" such as the "hyper-trophied magnificence" of the modern bathroom and the fashion for the continuous glass envelope of what he called the "aquarium staircase," he wrote with some surprise that: "In spite of precedent and ancestry, there is an undoubted new look about many of these houses: perhaps in the mere amount of window in some examples and the large use of curved metal tubing and railings. It used to be the aim of ship designers to make their interiors look as like as possible to long-shore buildings, with dummy fireplaces to preserve the illusion of stability: it now appears, *per contra*, to be the desire of some architects to

LEFT High Cross, William Lescaze's uncompromising new house for the headmaster of Dartington School, Devon, was a potent symbol of change, as well as being an effective advertisement for the metal windows of Crittall & Co.

LEFT Rational dress for the modern girl in her modern home: trouser outfits by couturier Paul Poiret, illustrated here by Georges Lepape in 1911. The inspiration for many of Poiret's clothes was Bakst's costume designs for the Ballets Russes.

make their houses look like ships, perhaps to create the feeling of rushing air and sunny decks. Streamlinism is a modern movement reflected equally in clothes and locomotives, and in an indefinite way connected with the cult of fitness."

Abercrombie was describing the Art Deco house, although he didn't know it at the time. If you were British in the 1930s, you might describe the Art Deco house as "modernistic," "jazz modern," or "streamlinist." And you would probably curl your lip slightly when you uttered the words, since you were more than likely to agree with the critic who condemned all the vulgar makers of "jazz-modern shop fronts in chromium plate and glass, all the purveyors of smart angular furniture and all the builders of nasty 'modernistic' villas."

An Australian might characterize it as "modern ship style;" an American as "streamline modern" or "liner style," "zigzag modern," or "skyscraper style," depending on its shape or size and his or her ability to register the nuances. If you were French, you would talk of "le style moderne," "le style 25," or "universalisme." And if, as an English-speaker, you wanted to impress with your sophistication and cosmopolitanism,

you might add a Gallic "e" to "modern," and refer to "jazz moderne," "streamline moderne," or "zigzag moderne."

Ironically, the name you would *not* give to such a building was "Art Deco." The label was virtually unknown until 1966, when the Musée des Arts Décoratifs in Paris used a shortened version of the title of the 1925 Exposition des Arts Décoratifs et Industriels Modernes for its exhibition "Les Années '25' Art Déco/Bauhaus/ Stijl/Esprit Nouveau." The phrase was brought to the notice of a wider public in 1968, when the British cultural historian Bevis Hillier adopted it for the title of his book *Art Deco of the 20s and 30s*; and had gained popular currency by November 1970, when *Art and Antiques Weekly* ran a long article celebrating the style, while at the same time expressing anxiety about its ultimate worth. The more traditional labels were relegated to confusing subdivisions of Deco, leading one critic to say that "there will have to be some agreement about nomenclature before any of us get much further;" and "Art Deco" was confirmed as the definitive term for the movement when Hillier curated a major exhibition with this title at the Minneapolis Institute of Arts in 1971.

LEFT Frank Lloyd Wright's Hollyhock House in Los Angeles was designed in 1917, when his work was being influenced by native American themes.

ABOVE The Palazzo della Civiltà Italiana near Rome, by Guerrini, La Padula, and Romano (1938–43). The design reflects one interwar perspective on classicism.

So Art Deco is a recent cultural construct. Moreover it is a sublimely elusive construct, for it continues to evolve, and after three decades of change it still manages to conceal more than it reveals. What, apart from the fact that they all date from the mid-1920s and are all routinely labelled as "Art Deco," really connects a street like the Rue Mallet-Stevens in Paris with a swan-shaped silver sauceboat from the Orfèvrerie Christofle, an ultra-streamlined piece of graphic art by Cassandre, and a Maurice Dufrêne sofa upholstered in bright geometrical tapestry? What links an expensive, elitist, and rather conservative lemonwood table by André Fréchet with a Moderne filling station in Los Angeles?

It makes more sense to consider Art Deco as an evolving network of tendencies and motifs rather than a coherent movement with a leader, a manifesto, and an ideological program. Its greatest achievement, apart from the production of some extraordinarily beautiful objects, was to mediate expertly between the avant-garde and tradition, which is a polite way of saying that it fed off other styles and movements, absorbing their most saleable features and spitting out the rest. So, for example, acknowledged ancestors include the opulent, angular lines of Josef Hoffmann's Palais Stoclet in Brussels (1905–11); the equally opulent interiors of other Wiener Werkstätte stalwarts such as Dagobert Peche and Koloman Moser; the works of Charles Rennie Mackintosh, such as the Glasgow School of Art (1897–9, 1907–9); and the sinuous, slightly shocking curves of Art Nouveau. It also took the forms and the cachet of German Modernism, without bothering much about the morality that underpinned them.

In its early incarnations Art Deco was a distinctively French invention, despite its cosmopolitan roots. The 1900 Exposition Universelle in Paris had established Art Nouveau as the dominant decorative style in Europe, and

France as its acknowledged master. However, the
1900 Exposition proved to be Art Nouveau's
swansong; within a decade its popularity had
dwindled almost to nothing, and first the Wiener
Werkstätte, then the Deutscher Werkbund,
demonstrated that Germany and Austria had
outstripped France as European leaders in design.
Inspired by the Société des Artistes Décorateurs,
which had been established in 1901 in the wake of
the Exposition Universelle, French craftsmen were
searching for a style that would restore their pre-
eminence. It was out of this that Art Deco began
to emerge as an identifiable tendency immediately
before World War I, in the designs of couturiers
such as Paul Poiret and Jacques Doucet, the early
furniture of Jacques-Emile Ruhlmann, and the
interiors of *ensembliers* such as Charlotte
Chauchet-Guilleré and Théodore Lambert, both
associated with the Atelier Primavera, which was
founded by the department store Le Printemps in
1913. After the disruption caused by the war, they
resumed that search, eschewing the high ideals
that motivated the Arts and Crafts movement in
Britain and the United States, but accepting its
emphasis on hand-crafted goods. Like Arts and
Crafts architects and designers, they looked to the
past for inspiration – particularly to the eighteenth
century, France's golden age of design.

In this first phase, which lasted until the mid-
1920s, Art Deco was built on deeply conservative
foundations – and it showed. The predominant
style in early twentieth-century France was the
kind of rational neo-classicism preached by Julian
Guadet and the Ecole des Beaux-Arts; even when
pioneers such as Auguste Perret and Tony Garnier
tried to break with tradition through their use of
new materials such as reinforced concrete, they
still thought in terms of redefining and reinventing
classical forms. One can see this classicism at
work in the interiors designed by leading French
ensembliers and many of their British
counterparts from 1910 right up until the 1930s.
Fréchet's salon of 1925 is one example that can
serve for many. The ivory-colored pilaster strips,
which punctuate the dark-grey walls, may
dispense with the capitals that a true classical
order demands. The fluting may be confined,
rather perversely, to their sides rather than the
surfaces that face into the room, and the dentils of
the cornice may be big, blocky, and stylized. But
the careful symmetry of Fréchet's design and the
proportions of the salon still exude an inescapable
breath of "Bozarts."

But Deco also borrowed the latest thing from
contemporary culture, and the more exotic and
foreign the latest thing was, the better. Japan, still

something of a novelty, even though it was seventy years since Matthew Perry had opened up trade with the west, was popular in the 1920s, and Parisian decorators learned lacquerwork at the feet of Japanese masters. In 1909 Serge Diaghilev's Ballets Russes took Paris by storm, and were a wild success in Europe throughout the 1910s and 1920s. The bright colors and alien, almost barbarous forms that set designer Lev Bakst and those who followed him used to define the ballet gave new impetus in France to the graphic arts, fashion, and interior design. And this extended to Britain. Robert Graves and Alan Hodge, in *The Long Week-end* (1940), a history of the inter-war years, describe how the typical post-war interior, with its walls of bluish-grey distemper, white woodwork, pseudo-Jacobean furniture, pale-green carpet and curtains of lilac-colored silk, was disturbed in 1919 "by cushions and hangings in startling 'jazz' patterns – influenced by Russian Ballet décor – 'futuristic' lamp shades, [and] huge ridiculous ornaments to make guests laugh."

Then there was Africa. France's love affair with African-American culture, in the shape of jazz, Josephine Baker, and the Revue Nègre at the Théâtre des Champs-Elysées, merged almost imperceptibly with racist and imperialist attitudes. In the early 1930s Egypt, Liberia, and Abyssinia were the only independent states in Africa (and Mussolini annexed the last in 1935): French colonial holdings at the time were considerable, and included Algeria, Tunisia, Senegambia, French Guinea, Dahomey, French Sudan, French Equatorial Africa, Madagascar, and French Somaliland. So-called "tribal" art – carvings, paintings, and the brightly colored geometrical patterns of North African textiles – all had an impact on French Art Deco, as did exotic and romantic images of the peoples of Africa and its flora and fauna. Interest in Africa culminated in the Exposition Coloniale Internationale, which took place in Paris in 1931 and was the biggest international exhibition in French history.

The past was just as much a foreign country as Japan, Russia, or Africa. On November 29, 1922, Howard Carter and the Earl of Carnarvon opened the tomb of the boy pharaoh Tutankhamun in Egypt's Valley of the Kings. With the discovery of

LEFT Robert Mallet-Stevens's contribution to the Ambassade Française, a design for a French embassy, exhibited at the 1925 Paris Exposition. Compare this with André Fréchet's restrained salon, shown on page 6; Mallet-Stevens was a leading figure in the Modernist wing of French Art Deco.

Making YESTERDAY'S BATHROOMS *fit for* TOMORROW

HERE'S A remodeling idea that really works wonders . . . the use of lovely polished walls of Carrara Structural Glass to bring outmoded bathrooms and kitchens up-to-date. Carrara's color-tones are soft and mellow, its beauty ageless, its charm and freshness simply preserved by an occasional wiping with a dampened cloth. Old rooms, grown worn and unattractive with time, literally take on new life when given a Carrara beauty treatment . . . while bathrooms and kitchens in new homes are certain to be truly distinctive if attired in walls of Carrara. Loveliness, permanence and utility . . . these are Carrara's important contributions to gracious homes and pleasant living.

THESE walls, done in the modern manner with Black and Ivory Carrara, could make any bathroom beautiful. And what bathroom, no matter how decrepit, wouldn't respond gaily to these two lovely Flesh Tinted Mirrors? Upper walls and ceiling of this room are finished in harmonious shades of quick-drying Wallhide Paint.

CARRARA
>>> *The modern structural glass* <<<

CLIP THE COUPON FOR FREE BOOKLET
PITTSBURGH
PLATE GLASS COMPANY
2234A Grant Bldg., Pittsburgh, Pa.
Please send me, without obligation, your new book entitled "Personality Bathrooms and Character Kitchens"
Name . . . .
Address . . . .
City . . . . State . . . .

ABOVE "Hyper-trophied magnificence" crosses the Atlantic: the bathroom in this American advertisement, which appeared in a 1935 issue of *Fortune* magazine, shows the influence of the French designer Francis Jourdain. The walls are clad in colored glass.

RIGHT A salon by the master of French Art Deco, Jacques-Emile Ruhlmann, from the *Répertoire du goût moderne* (1928–9). By this time Ruhlmann's work was moving hesitantly towards a more rectilinear modernism.

the untouched inner chamber the following February, and the exhumation of Tutankhamun's mummy, a wave of enthusiasm for all things ancient Egyptian swept the western world. The porches of suburban bungalows in California were supported by papyrus columns, while the lapels of chic Parisian socialites were adorned with jeweled scarabs. When "Tutmania" was at its height, sphinxes looked down on crowded dance halls, hieroglyphics covered the foyers of movie houses, and the lounges of luxury liners were decked out with references to Ra and Osiris.

This interest in past civilizations as sources for a new design vocabulary extended beyond ancient Egypt. The stepped-back shape of the Sumerian ziggurat was a recurring motif; and one can see it in the most unlikely places, of which Newbury, in England, where Thomas S. Tait adapted the form for a suburban villa, is one of the oddest. It was adopted by Deco architects sometimes for its exoticism, sometimes for its practicality as a means of accommodating a large number of offices or apartments (Henri Sauvage's unexecuted scheme for sixteen-story apartment-ziggurats on the River Seine in Paris is a case in point), and sometimes simply because urban zoning laws stipulated that high-rise buildings must be stepped back to allow sunlight into the streets below.

Art Deco's voracious appetite for alien cultures led to some strange bedfellows. Inextricably linked to the ziggurat, for example, was the indigenous American culture of the Aztecs and Mayans. Frank Lloyd Wright, who, after Ernest Wasmuth published in Berlin in 1910 his portfolio of Wright's *Studies and Executed Buildings*, was himself a massive influence on architecture and European design in the 1910s and 1920s, stimulated interest in Mayan and native American design. The Los Angeles house that he designed for Aline Barnsdale in 1917 was decorated with motifs derived from Mayan art, while its living room has a stylized overmantel panel depicting his client as an enthroned Indian queen looking out over above the deserts of southern California to the rocky tablelands beyond.

High Deco reached its peak in the famous 1925 Paris Exposition that eventually gave the movement its name. France's leading designers all took part, from *ensembliers* and furniture makers such as Ruhlmann, Fréchet, and Chauchet-Guilleré to more avant-garde figures such as Robert Mallet-Stevens and Pierre Chareau. Between them they showed the world that France had succeeded in creating a new design vocabulary, albeit an amorphous and eclectic one, which was able to encompass set-piece interiors as diverse as a magnificent woman's bedroom in white maple featured by Maurice Dufrêne – a study in traditional sybaritic living, all silks and polar bear skins – and aggressively rectilinear compositions such as George Champion's black-and-yellow dining room. The keynote was luxury: unusual materials, exotic woods, and individually hand-crafted pieces. The High Deco that epitomized French design by 1925 was not for the man and woman in the street.

The world came to marvel at France's achievement. Many of the architects whose work features in the following pages made the pilgrimage to Paris in 1925: Berthold Lubetkin and Oliver Hill; Amyas Connell and Basil Ward; Wells Coates, Ernest Cormier, Serge Chermayeff.

American designers also visited the Exposition. Walter Dorwin Teague, the "Dean of Industrial Design," deserted the florid, grotesque ornament in which his Madison Avenue advertising agency specialized and began to develop a much more streamlined, shiny, modernist look. And Donald Deskey, the industrial designer who is usually credited with developing Streamline Moderne as a distinctively American variant of Art Deco, was inspired to start business as a design consultant in New York after seeing the Exposition.

Ironically enough, the fair proved to be High Art Deco's finest hour. By 1930 French Deco was already an ageing whore: unfaithful, avaricious, and desperately trying to stay young by giving itself to the latest trend. Tired of its superficiality, its best designers – Eileen Gray, Ruhlmann, Chareau, Mallet-Stevens – began to experiment with materials that, while still exotic, were markedly less traditional than the expensive woods and natural fabrics that had once figured so prominently. Chrome, glass, and tubular steel replaced ivory-encrusted macassar ebony, Indies rosewood, and Gabonese bilinga; austere white

LEFT Our Mayan in Havana: a Deco apartment block in Cuba's capital, designed by the Cuban architect Eugenio Rayneri Piedra.

walls and abstract geometric patterns replaced damask hangings and figurative tapestries. The Société des Artistes Décorateurs, which now seemed staid and outmoded, gave way to the Union des Artistes Modernes, whose members rejected extravagant ornament in favor of functionalism and modernism.

The major architectural monuments of Art Deco are all public or commercial buildings rather than private residences. One only has to think of New York skyscrapers such as the Chrysler Building (William van Alen, 1928–31) and Shreve, Lamb & Harmon's Empire State Building (1930–1), or that city's Radio City Music Hall, with its interiors by Deskey (1932–3). The same can be said of London's Art Deco icons: the streamlined, black-vitrolite exterior of Owen Williams's Daily Express Building on Fleet Street (1930–2); the sweeping

lines of F.E. Bromige's Grosvenor Cinema in Rayners Lane (1936); the Hoover Factory in Perivale by Wallis Gilbert and Partners (1932).

Art Deco was primarily concerned with the decorative arts and interior design. Surface was all; structure and shape merely the pegs on which to hang decoration. But many of Deco's leading designers were also architects, and Art Deco architecture continued the habit of borrowing – often the best, occasionally the worst, but always the most theatrical – from other cultures, countries, and contemporaneous movements. As a result, one can find in Art Deco buildings elements of De Stijl, of Frank Lloyd Wright's Mayan phase, of Italian Futurism and German Expressionism, and even of Russian Constructivism. The neo-classicism that played such an important role in the evolution of French Deco also remained a potent force, in the guise of "stripped classical," which made use of the basic forms but not the ornament of classicism.

The movement that had the greatest impact on Art Deco buildings was undoubtedly Modernism. The rationalist aesthetic of Peter Behrens, Adolf Loos, the Bauhaus, and Le Corbusier emphasized functionalism, mass production, and prefabrication, and the vital role of the architect in creating better buildings for a better society. None of these things was of particular interest to Deco architects, who continued to deal in the superficial at the expense of the ideological. But by the 1920s, the Modernist aesthetic had developed a vocabulary of its own; one that made use of different building materials – steel, reinforced concrete, glass – and plain white surfaces, rectangular volumes, and flat roofs; one that dispensed with historical elements, broke down conventional distinctions between interior and exterior spaces, and dwelled at great length on the importance of sunshine and fresh air for healthy living.

It was these *visual* elements that the builders of the Art Deco house really took to their hearts. Such elements were leavened with the occasional curved bay window, with gleaming metal rails surrounding a roof terrace, cantilevered canopies, and vast expanses of tinted glass. But then the purest Modernist wasn't above such devices. And if a little ornament crept in here and there – a panel with a sunburst or some zigzag carving in relief, some stained glass, a set of streamlined parallel lines painted a different color from the rest of the wall – that was hardly the end of the world. After all, no one, not even the purists, wanted to live in a factory; and the cool, futuristic vision of the house as a technological paradise must be mediated to some extent by individuality and comfort, by traditional, non-functionalist ideas of home. Life should be fun. And it was.

LEFT Cantilevers and reinforced concrete become pure poetry in the Penguin Pool at London Zoo (1934), by Berthold Lubetkin and Tecton. Ramps were a popular feature of avant-garde houses of the 1920s and 1930s, although humans rarely used them to such effect.

When, in Evelyn Waugh's novel *Decline and Fall* (1928), the delightfully capricious Margot Beste-Chetwynde decides to demolish her country house, King's Thursday – "the finest piece of domestic Tudor in England" – and replace it with "something clean and square," she paves the way for one of the greatest architectural creations in twentieth-century literature. Her young architect, Professor Silenus, is every inch the Corbusian Modernist: for him, the only perfect building is the factory, because it is designed to house machines rather than human beings. The problem of all art, he tells a journalist, is "the elimination of the human element from the consideration of form."

And yet when Silenus's new King's Thursday is built, it turns out to be very different from the super-functional machine for living in that he first envisaged. Although it is indeed a colossal ferro-concrete mansion, the Professor, as one of the other characters in the novel comments, has "got right away from Le Corbusier." There are aluminium blinds shading windows of vita-glass; a terrace of silver and scarlet paving; a bathroom with a sunken malachite bath; and a dining room with a vulcanite dining table. The hall floor is made of bottle-green glass, Margot Beste-Chetwynde's study has a luminous ceiling and her drawing room floor is a large kaleidoscope which operates by electricity. In fact, King's Thursday has evolved into an Art Deco house. All it needs for perfection is a few Marion Dorn rugs, a lacquered Eileen Gray daybed, and some of the impossibly opulent pieces shown by Ruhlmann, Dunand, and Chareau at the 1925 Paris Exposition.

The path from Modern to Moderne was a well-trodden one – particularly for patrons who, like Mrs Beste-Chetwynde, began by aspiring to "something clean and square," only to discover that what they really wanted was avant-garde but sumptuous decoration which would reflect their status and artistic tastes without condemning them to a life of fashionable but uncomfortable

PREVIOUS PAGE The Butler House, des Moines, Iowa, by Kraetsch & Kraetsch, 1934–6.

BELOW Images like this, part of a stained-glass panel by Ricardo Leone (1935), promoted a sophisticated Hollywood-inspired lifestyle which was entirely out of reach for most consumers.

RIGHT Screen by Léon Jallot and his son Maurice. Léon, who showed interiors at the 1925 Paris Exposition, moved towards Modernism, abstract patterns, and new materials in the later 1920s.

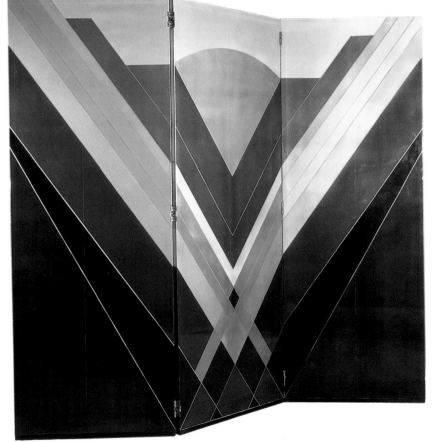

white-walled austerity. And it was the Margot Beste-Chetwyndes of the world who were the major clients for the Art Deco house and its offspring; people who were fast and rich; prone to superficialities; often whimsical to the point of eccentricity; and, above all, cosmopolitan.

Their choice of architecture was also cosmopolitan in the true sense of the word: it was without national limitations; it belonged to every part of the world. Henry-Russell Hitchcock is usually credited with coining the phrase "international style" in his 1929 book *Modern Architecture, Romanticism and Reintegration*, although he was using the term restrictively, referring specifically to the functional Modernism of Le Corbusier and Gropius, Gerrit Rietveld, and Mies van der Rohe. In the process he hijacked the concept of a cosmopolitan architectural style. Art Deco – especially the later, more streamlined form of Deco which was developing as Hitchcock was writing – was just as global, just as heedless of local vernacular as any building by Mies van der Rohe or Le Corbusier. If it sometimes owed its internationalism to the rise of Hollywood, and if it occasionally lacked the moral earnestness of the

International Style proper, it could also be a lot more fun than its purist contemporary.

If proof of this were needed, it can be found in the eclectic group of houses included in this chapter, all designed between 1929 and 1937. Within that short period we see romantic Modernism in Germany and suburban Deco in New Zealand, High Deco interiors near Detroit and in central India, and Streamline Moderne masterpieces in Iowa, Australia, and Dublin.

ABOVE Bold patterns make this 1930s showcase interior by an unidentified designer rather unsettling to the eye.

BELOW Art Deco's curves and concrete canopies, as in this example in Cape Town, South Africa, appealed to city dwellers all over the world.

THE HOUSE
OF TOMORROW

NORMAN BEL GEDDES, 1931

Given the delightful air of unreality that pervades Art Deco architecture, it is fitting that the first house in this book should be an unrealized fantasy project. Norman Bel Geddes (1893–1958) started out as a theater designer in New York in 1918. He opened his own industrial design studio in 1927 and soon established a reputation as a brilliant but eccentric creator of everything from furniture and wireless sets to a streamlined train, a teardrop-shaped car, and a futuristic airplane.

However, many of Bel Geddes's other designs never reached production, not least because of his cheerful disregard for the practicalities of industrial manufacture. The House of Tomorrow was one of a number of projects from the early 1930s that showed his commitment to an aesthetic that discarded precedent and tradition, and belonged entirely to the future. The ramps and terraces, sweeping lines, and provocative geometric curves all demonstrate how much American Deco owed to the avant-garde architecture of Russian Constructivists such as Iakov Chernikov and Konstantin Melnikov.

There were plenty of other idealistic Houses of Tomorrow in the 1930s. A high point of the Chicago Centennial World's Fair of 1933, for example, was a Street of Tomorrow containing twelve houses, each expressing a different designer's vision of the future. There were walls made of glass blocks; a Cypress House built entirely of cypress wood; and another of corrugated steel faced with porcelain panels. But the exhibit that attracted most interest was William and George Keck's twelve-sided House of Tomorrow, complete with central air-conditioning, a built-in dishwasher, and electrically operated doors to its two garages – one for the family car and the other for the family airplane.

Bel Geddes's finest hour came with the 1939 New York World's Fair, which had the theme "The World of Tomorrow." He was commissioned to design the General Motors pavilion, named Highways and Horizons but better known today as Futurama – a model of America in 1960 measuring 3340 square meters (36,000 square feet). Visitors sat in moving chairs, each equipped with its own individual loudspeaker, while they gazed in awe at futuristic homes and cities filled with skyscrapers, floating airship hangars, and a vast complex of superhighways. On leaving, everyone was given a small blue-and-white pin bearing the legend "I have seen the future." Ironically, for he was vehemently anti-capitalist, Bel Geddes had defined corporate America's vision of a world of consumerism, materialism, and profit.

ABOVE AND OPPOSITE **Norman Bel Geddes shows a detail of his World of Tomorrow to enthusiastic General Motors executives, and his prescription for how that plan would be realised.**

BELOW **"I have seen the future" – Bel Geddes's model of the House of Tomorrow is a marvelously sculptural composition, merging Constructivism with Streamline Moderne.**

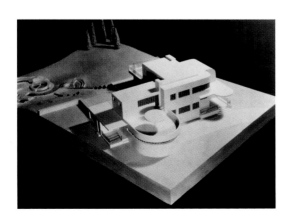

THE PRICE of the HOME JOURNAL

PUBLISHED once a month, 10c the copy. By subscription: To the United States and Possessions, Canada and Newfoundland (including Labrador), $1.00 the year; $1.50 for 2 years; $2.00 for 3 years. Remit by Post Office or Express Money Order, Check or by Draft payable in United States or Canadian Funds.

To Argentina, Bolivia, Brazil, Chile, Colombia, Costa Rica, Cuba, Dominican Republic, Ecuador, Guatemala, Haiti, Isle of Pines, Mexico, Nicaragua, Panama, Paraguay, Peru, Republic of Honduras, Salvador, Spain, Uruguay and Venezuela, $1.00 the year. To other countries, $2.50 the year. Remittance to be by Postal or Express Money Order or by Draft payable in United States Funds. Single copies a shilling *anywhere in England.*

Ladies'
HOME JOURNAL
(THE HOME JOURNAL)

THE FAMILY MAGAZINE OF AMERICA
Registered in the United States Patent Office and in Foreign Countries

PUBLISHED ON THE THIRD TUESDAY OF
THE MONTH PRECEDING ITS DATE BY

**THE CURTIS
PUBLISHING
COMPANY**

INDEPENDENCE SQUARE
PHILADELPHIA, PENNSYLVANIA

CYRUS H. K. CURTIS, *President*
GEORGE H. LORIMER, *First Vice-President*
JOHN B. WILLIAMS, *Second Vice-President*
WALTER D. FULLER
Second Vice-President and Secretary
PHILIP S. COLLINS
Second Vice-President and Treasurer
FRED A. HEALY
Second Vice-President and Advertising Director

LORING A. SCHULER, *Editor*

CHESLA C. SHERLOCK, STUART O. BLYTHE, RICHARD E. MYERS, W. J. DE GROUCHY, LITA BANE, MARGUERITE ASPINWALL, GRAEME LORIMER, J. HAROLD HAWKINS, LOIS PALMER, *Associate Editors*

Copyright, 1930 (trade-mark registered), by The Curtis Publishing Company, in the United States and Great Britain. London Offices, 6, Henrietta Street, Covent Garden, W. C. All rights reserved. Entered as second class matter May 6, 1911, at the Post Office at Philadelphia, Pa., under Act of March 3, 1879. Additional entry at Columbus, O., Chicago, Ill., Indianapolis, Ind., San Francisco, Cal., Seattle, Wash., Houston, Tex., Des Moines, Ia., Los Angeles, Cal., St. Louis, Mo., Saginaw, Mich., Milwaukee, Wis., St. Paul, Minn., Kansas City, Mo., Savannah, Ga., Denver, Colo., Portland, Ore., Louisville, Ky., Omaha, Neb., Ogden, Utah, Jacksonville, Fla., New Orleans, La., Portland, Me., Detroit, Mich., Cleveland, O.

Ten Years From Now

By NORMAN BEL GEDDES

EDITOR'S NOTE—Norman Bel Geddes is looked upon today as one of the most daring yet practical originators of new ideas. After a successful beginning as a portrait painter of Enrico Caruso, Brand Whitlock, Ernestine Schumann-Heink and others, and as a stage designer of such productions as Erminie, Lady Be Good, Eugene O'Neill's Lazarus Laughed, The Miracle, Fifty Million Frenchmen and Lysistrata, Mr. Geddes turned his talents to industrial problems. His belief that the stupid and ugly cannot be functionally superior is now being proved in everything in the industrial world from beds to buildings.

It was because of his great interest in social and industrial innovations that we asked him to forecast for JOURNAL readers some of the changes of the next ten years.

ALL the following prophecies will be old-fashioned.

Aluminum will replace steel in railroad-car construction.

There will be double-deck streets, divided into lanes for slow stop-off traffic and lanes for express traffic.

Synthetic materials will replace the products of Nature in buildings.

Arc welding will replace riveting.

Every roof will be a garden.

Airplanes will be able to land and take off vertically. Whole blocks, in the midst of cities, will be given over to airplane hangars, the roofs of which will form landing fields.

Exterior walls of buildings will be of thinner material to effect economy of space.

Houses, in all climates, will have flat roofs.

Every floor will have one or more terraces.

So that such terraces shall not cut off light from the floor below, even small houses will be built with setbacks, as are skyscrapers today.

The garage will be part of the house and will be placed on the street front.

Service quarters will be at the front of the house; living rooms at the back.

All metal used in house construction will be so alloyed or treated as to render it noncorrosive.

In small houses the dining room, as a separate chamber, will be eliminated.

Houses, in the main, will tend to be smaller, but the fewer rooms they will contain will be larger.

All rooms will be soundproof.

Steel for building will be replaced by another alloy of half the weight but equal strength.

Neon tubes will replace the incandescent lamp.

Windows, while admitting violet rays, will not open.

All dwellings will be ventilated by artificial means; washed air, heated or cooled according to the season, will be delivered from a central plant.

The home will become so mechanized that handwork will be reduced to a minimum.

Mechanical devices, controlled by the photoelectric cell, will open doors, serve meals, and remove dirty dishes and clothes to the appropriate departments in the building.

A combination dictaphone and typewriter will eliminate the stenographer.

Talking pictures will replace talking professors.

Courses and lectures will be broadcast by television from key cities to hundreds of rural branches.

Talking motion pictures will achieve a third-dimensional quality.

Events of national interest will be available to you by television simultaneously with their occurrence.

It will be possible, through the medium of television, to hear and see the great artists of the world in your own home.

The present-day railroad sleeping car will have disappeared. All space will be divided into individual compartments of various sizes.

DECORATION BY EARL HORTER

Electricity will replace steam on Eastern railroads extending as far as Chicago.

Aircraft will attain a speed of six miles per minute.

A network of airlines will encircle the globe, supplementing our present transport facilities and tapping remote regions now little known to civilized man.

Aircraft will be provided with sleeping compartments and dining salons.

A new fuel of vastly increased power but of infinitesimal bulk will supersede gasoline.

Application of aerodynamics to automobile body design will increase performance per horse power by lessening wind resistance.

Engine and transmission in automobiles will be in one unit, placed at the rear of the machine.

There will be no epidemics.

There will be no incurable diseases.

Medical and surgical treatment will reduce crime to a fraction of its present-day proportion.

A Commercial League of Nations will regulate international commerce. So, there will be no slumps—no booms.

The working week will consist of four six-hour days.

Improvement in machinery will free workers from the drudgery of purely mechanical human tasks.

Women's dresses will be shorter; women's dresses will be longer; women's dresses will be shorter; then, women's dresses will be longer.

Men's clothing will be rational, comfortable—and much criticized.

Synthetic materials will supplement wool and cotton in the manufacture of clothing.

Artists will be thinking in terms of the industrial problems of their age.

Utilitarian objects will be as beautiful as what we call today "works of art."

Music and musical instruments will be revolutionized and given immeasurable new resources by the division of the whole tone into sixteenths instead of the present-day halves.

The "Color Organ" will definitely take its place as a recognized medium of expression.

The speaking stage will take on a more specialized form, comparable to symphony concerts today.

Talking pictures will take the place of the theater as we know it today.

Rainfall will be controlled scientifically.

Crops will be artificially stimulated by scientific methods.

All farms will be run on a coöperative basis with their own marketing and distributing facilities.

The world's literature will be available at ten cents a copy.

Paper will be replaced by material which does not depend upon the slow growth of trees for its production.

Today's small talk will have disappeared—only to be replaced by the equally unimportant 1940 brand.

Manipulation of lights will entirely eliminate scenery in the theater.

Exploration of the sea bottom and of interplanetary space will make possible the absolute prediction of weather conditions.

The power of ocean tides will be harnessed to serve us.

We will still be wishing one another "Happy New Year."

There will still be cruelty and intolerance. There will still be generosity and unselfishness. There will still be workers and drones.

In other words, there will still be—men and women.

VILLA SCHMINKE

HANS SCHAROUN, 1932–3

OPPOSITE While many of Scharoun's contemporaries were focusing their energies on producing angular, rectilinear architecture, his predilection for rounded corners and sweeping curves made Villa Schminke stand out from the Modernist mainstream.

V illa Schminke, at Löbau in Saxony, about 16km (10 miles) from Germany's border with the Czech Republic, rarely rates more than a passing mention in the standard architectural histories of the twentieth century. Yet it is one of the most exciting houses of the interwar years, a brilliant example of how architects could break out of the Modernist box without retreating into the past or pursuing novelty for its own sake.

Hans Scharoun (1893–1972), who designed the house, was born in Bremen and studied architecture from 1912 to 1914 at the Technische Hochschule in Berlin. After World War I he worked on reconstruction projects in East Prussia, while also becoming involved in the Gläserne Kette, or "Glass Chain," of Expressionist architects that formed around the German architect and polemicist Bruno Taut. Like Taut, he produced a number of visionary designs that stood no chance of ever being executed: "fantastic buildings for imprecisely formulated purposes," as one recent writer put it.

In 1925 Scharoun was appointed professor at the Akademie für Kunst und Kunstgewerbe in Breslau, where he also set up in practice; and the following year he became one of the twenty-seven members of Der Ring, a Berlin-based organization of architects that included Taut, Walter Gropius, Mies van der Rohe, Peter Behrens, and Erich Mendelsohn. Der Ring's objective was to make a stand against the conservative architectural establishment of the day, "to struggle against impractical and bureaucratic resistance for the establishment of a new concept of building."

By allying himself with the German avant-garde, Scharoun – who, like many in Der Ring, was a socialist – acquired a reputation as one of the nation's most exciting functionalist architects. His name was on everyone's lips (often coupled with that of Mies van der Rohe), and to the radicals, he was a man from whom great things were expected. "Expected" is the key word here, because for most of the 1920s Scharoun built very little. His reputation rested on his teaching, some imaginative but impractical competition entries, and the occasional impenetrable pronouncement.

In 1927 Scharoun designed an experimental single-family housing unit for the Werkbund exhibition at Stuttgart-Weissenhof; and through the influence of Martin Wagner, a member of Der Ring and Berlin's municipal architect, he designed or collaborated on several of the *Siedlungen*, or residential settlements, of the late 1920s, notably Siemensstadt in Berlin, where he contributed apartment buildings and the overall site plan. Scharoun's apartments were simple one- and two-bedroomed units, but he departed from pure functionalism in the dramatic variety of window types he used and in his curved, projecting staircase turrets, which make his designs

ABOVE Villa Schminke's steel-frame construction enabled Scharoun to break out of the box in a way that Frank Lloyd Wright never imagined, by making the flat planes of the house walls subordinate to the spaces that interrupt them.

seem at once more sculptural and less regimented than those of his co-workers at Siemensstadt, Gropius and Fred Forbat. He was criticized for his inability to put Expressionism behind him: the dwelling he exhibited at the Werkbund show was censured by the Dutch theorist Theo van Doesburg because of the "aesthetical treatments of ceiling, walls, and details, considered odious according to functionalist ideas." For the truth was that Scharoun still retained a romantic fascination with the more whimsical aspects of Expressionism. If ornament was no longer considered appropriate, then he considered it perfectly acceptable to create variety and to beautify through the manipulation of space and its boundaries. A socially responsible approach to modern architecture did not necessarily mean the creation of boring boxes.

Villa Schminke demonstrates just how whimsical Scharoun could be. Built around a steel frame, it deliberately spurns the pure functional box, with curves breaking out everywhere. One's first impression is of its essential oddness. The lack of corners, right angles – even walls – is deeply unsettling. It disturbs our ideas of what a house should be. Plane surfaces are broken with narrow strips of window; they erupt into sloping glass walls; and most of all they simply disappear, to be replaced by voids between steel columns and the spaces created by a spectacular series of curved balconies that project at seemingly random angles from the main block. Inside, sunlight pours through the house, while the internal walls – in the form of moveable screens and curtains – are constantly shifting, again confounding our ideas of the home as a fixed, static space.

The balconies are the most dramatic feature. Supported on freestanding columns, they give the building a sense of openness and light, and their refusal to admit a single, sharp, ninety-degree angle suggests a deeply organic response to domestic architecture. The house has soft, asymmetric lines, as if an ocean liner has been planted in the soil of Saxony. This reference to liners in one of Europe's most landlocked areas is surely playful, ironic – a glorious example of postmodernism in an age when Modernism itself was still young.

Despite his left-wing politics, Scharoun stayed in Germany when the Nazis came to power in 1933. He saw Der Ring forced to disband and Modernism condemned as degenerate; he watched as Taut went to Japan, Mendelsohn and Gropius to England, and Mies van der Rohe eventually to Chicago. Scharoun eked out a living building private houses with pitched roofs and conventional exteriors – although as Peter Blundell Jones, a leading authority on the architect, points out, these "reveal an extreme spatial fluidity inside … in them he tested the spatial ideas found in his later work."

It was not until the late 1950s that Scharoun had the chance to live up to the reputation he had acquired thirty years earlier. His brand of organic functionalism finally came into fashion, and he received a string of commissions for major public buildings – the Romeo and Juliet apartments in Stuttgart (1956–9); the German Embassy in Brasilia (1963–9); the Berlin State Library (finished in 1978, six years after his death). His best work is widely held to be the Berlin Philharmonie; but Villa Schminke, with its curious, wedge-shaped balconies and its determination to break down conventional ideas about housing, is a neglected masterpiece of the twentieth century.

LEFT Sloping banks of glass ensure that the main living rooms are flooded with sunlight, while moveable screens create an internal plan which can be altered as required.

BURNHAM BEECHES

HARRY NORRIS FOR ALFRED NICHOLAS, 1933–4

Hollywood and the hedonism that, paradoxically, characterized the global economic depression of the early 1930s meant that Streamline Moderne spread rapidly round the world. The style offered a more flamboyant alternative to the extreme functionalism and ideological correctness of Modernism proper.

In Australia, Art Deco had already taken hold by the late 1920s. The American architect Walter Burley Griffin, who settled there in 1914, designed a number of interesting Deco buildings with strong Mayan Revival features, such as the City of Sydney Incinerator (with E.M. Nicholls) and the Capitol Theater, Melbourne (1926, with Marion Mahony Griffin). Melbourne, in particular, still has a fine collection of Deco and Deco-related architecture, from the Streamline Moderne of Alkira House (James Wardop, 1936) to the Snowcrete façade and Egyptian motifs of the Myer's department store (H.Q. & F.B. Tompkins, 1933) and the zigzags and flowers of Harry Norris's Block Court (1930), a shopping arcade inserted into a late-Victorian building.

BELOW Burnham Beeches is the masterpiece of the Melbourne architect Harry Norris and the crowning glory of the Modern Ship Style, as Streamline Moderne was known in Australia in the 1930s.

Norris seems to have specialized in commercial premises, and he is responsible for several Deco stores and offices in the heart of Melbourne. But he also turned his hand to country houses for wealthy industrialists. One of these is his masterpiece and perhaps the crowning glory of Australian Deco. Burnham Beeches, in the tiny town of Sherbrooke, about 35km (22 miles) from Melbourne, was built for Alfred Nicholas, who had started as a grocer and importer before joining his brother in 1917 as business manager for the pharmaceuticals firm G.R. Nicholas & Co. Nicholas became very rich, and in the early 1930s he commissioned Norris to design a home for him.

Norris and Nicholas opted for an exciting and uncompromising Streamline Moderne. "Walking up the drive at dusk," reported *The Australian Home Beautiful* in 1934, "one sees the towering bulk of a great grey battleship with turrets, masts and searchlight complete. From any viewpoint, however, it is unusual and extremely interesting." And so it is. A big house, Burnham Beeches is made to look even bigger by the tiers of railed and deck-like terraces, verandahs, and balconies that project from the main block, and the bright awnings, which protect the rooms within from the searing heat of the sun.

The central section was dominated by a spacious lounge, measuring 18m x 9m (60ft x 29ft), decorated in ivory and russets and with a jade carpet. This room was reached via an elliptical entrance hall, which rose the full height of the house with a sweeping iron staircase that wound its way up to what Nicholas called his "ambulatory" – a stepped-back, curved conning tower filled with vast expanses of plate glass from which the magnate could survey the surrounding Sherbrooke Forest.

Nicholas died in 1937, only a few years after the house was finished. It is now a hotel, but the extensive grounds are open to the public.

ABOVE A 1934 photograph of the house, showing the cantilevered entrance porch, the railed decks with their awnings, and the conning tower, which looked out over woodland.

BELOW The lounge filled the center of the house. There was a sun room at each end, and an open verandah (which lay to the right in this period photograph) ran the full length of the room.

MANIK BAGH

ECKART MUTHESIUS FOR THE MAHARAJAH OF INDORE, 1930–3

ABOVE Eckart Muthesius in about 1929, the year after he met Prince Yeshwant Rao Holkar Bahadur. Eckart's father-in-law, Marcel Hardy, was the Prince's tutor at Oxford.

BELOW The palace's garden façade. Muthesius originally proposed a much more Modernistic treatment with flat roofs and no traditional elements at all, but the Maharajah toned this down.

Despite various hesitant attempts at Moderne, in 1930 Indian architecture was still dominated by the British imperialistic values that had found expression in the vice-regal complex at New Delhi, designed by Edwin Lutyens and Herbert Baker and begun eighteen years earlier. But just as Lutyens's monumental Viceroy's House was completed in 1930, the twenty-two-year-old Prince Yeshwant Rao Holkar Bahadur became Maharajah of Indore, in central India. Educated at Charterhouse and Christ Church College, Oxford, the Maharajah was fabulously wealthy, a discriminating connoisseur, and a sophisticated patron of the European avant-garde. He was determined that Indore should adopt modern values; and his first step was to build a thoroughly modern residence.

There were already two palaces – one nineteenth-century and traditional, the other Lutyenesque-classical and recent – in the Maharajah's capital city, also called Indore, which lay about 480km (300 miles) east of Bombay. But he preferred something more suited to progressive western tastes and turned for help to an acquaintance from his Oxford days, the German architect Eckart Muthesius (1904–89), whose father-in-law had written the definitive account of turn-of-the-century English domestic architecture, *Das englische Haus*.

Eckart's design for what became Manik Bagh, or the Garden of Jewels, would have raised a few eyebrows in London or New York, never mind central India. (A 1930s English guidebook described the palace, in the state of Madhya Pradesh, simply as a "most conspicuous building.") Although there were some traditional elements, notably in the open loggias on the garden front, Muthesius made extensive use of white stucco and tinted glass in metal frames, and his deliberately simple treatment of exteriors and interiors set Manik Bagh apart from contemporary Indian architecture.

Muthesius designed some of the furnishings, including Modernist nickel-silver standard lamps and armchairs. Like a number of items in the palace, they were made to his specifications in Berlin and shipped out to India. However, the Maharajah had a taste for modern Parisian furniture: Ruhlmann supplied the palace with office furniture in chrome, red leather, and macassar ebony; a Transat chair by Eileen Gray stood in the Maharajah's bedroom; and at some point a chaise longue by Le Corbusier and Charlotte Perriand was purchased. Both the Maharajah and the Maharani slept in beds designed by Louis Sognot and Charlotte Alix; the Maharani's was a particularly fine piece, with a headboard of bright-green glass and shining chrome.

The Maharani died in 1937, aged twenty-one; and with her death the Maharajah lost his enthusiasm for modernity. He died in 1956. Manik Bagh remained in a near-perfect condition (and his family continued to live there) until the 1970s, when the Indian government's withdrawal of state subsidies from maharajahs forced them to sell. Today it houses Madhya Pradesh's Central Excise Commissariat.

SAARINEN HOUSE

ELIEL SAARINEN FOR HIMSELF, 1929–30

ABOVE Eliel Saarinen, photographed in 1931, in his role as architectural director at Cranbrook.

RIGHT The dining room. Saarinen designed the table and chairs, which were made by the Company of Master Craftsmen of New York. The wall hanging depicting a landscape is by Greta Skogster.

C ranbrook is recognized throughout the world as a remarkable experiment in the union of education, arts, and sciences. And one of the most remarkable things about it is Saarinen House, which, against all the odds, unites Arts and Crafts values and Art Deco design. The 127-hectare (315-acre) campus in Bloomfield Hills, Michigan, was the brainchild of a wealthy local newspaper magnate, George Gough Booth, who in 1904 bought a run-down farm as a summer retreat and named it Cranbrook, after the village in Kent, England, where his father had been born. Over the next forty years Booth and his wife Ellen transformed Cranbrook into a progressive educational community with a boys' school, a girls' school, kindergarten, meeting house, art academy, museum, and church.

The Booths' ideals were rooted firmly in the Arts and Crafts movement – George Gough Booth was founder and first president of the Detroit Society of Arts and Crafts – and the early buildings at Cranbrook, which were designed by his architect son Henry Scripps Booth and Albert Kahn, a friend of Booth senior and a fellow member of the Society, all show a touching

fidelity to English prototypes, complete with half-timbered gables, tall, mock-Tudor chimneystacks, and linen-fold paneling over the fireplace.

The Finnish architect Eliel Saarinen (1873–1950), who defined the architectural character of Cranbrook over almost a quarter of a century, was himself no stranger to the Arts and Crafts movement and its architecture of community. Heavily influenced by the British architects M.H. Baillie Scott and C.F.A. Voysey, he and his two partners, Herman Gesellius and Armas Lindgren, had built in 1902 an idealistic complex of residences and studios on a picturesque site overlooking Lake Vitträsk, near Helsinki. As an experiment in communal living, the Hvitträsk complex was disastrous: the bachelor Gesellius fell in love with Saarinen's wife Matti, who divorced her husband to marry him. On the same day Saarinen married Gesellius's sister Loja. The two women didn't speak, and the atmosphere was so tense that Lindgren soon left, to be followed by Gesellius and Matti. But as an essay in romantic and stylized vernacular, the complex was a resounding success. Although the Saarinens left for America in 1923, prompted by Eliel's winning of the second prize in an international competition to design the Chicago Tribune tower, they returned to Hvitträsk every summer.

Saarinen's association with Cranbrook began when he was living in Ann Arbor as Visiting Professor of Architecture at the University of Michigan. Henry Scripps Booth and Albert Kahn both had a high opinion of the Finn's abilities as an architect; and in the spring of 1925, inspired by a visit to the

American Academy in Rome, George Gough Booth asked him to produce "an idealistic plan" for an academy of art at Cranbrook. Saarinen came up with a scheme for a campus filled with towers and formal gardens, but this proved too ambitious for Booth, who didn't feel able to justify the massive expenditure it would have involved. Nevertheless, he liked what he saw, and when he decided to build a school to develop the spirit of democracy, which he optimistically supposed to be "inherent in American boyhood," he commissioned Saarinen to design it on the site of a dairy farm on the estate.

This was the first fruit of a fertile partnership. Eliel and Loja Saarinen moved to Bloomfield Hills in late 1925, and between 1926 and 1929 the Cranbook School for Boys went up, followed by a school for girls in 1930–1 and, between 1928 and 1942, the complex of buildings that eventually made up the Cranbrook Academy of Art. With such a quantity of work, Saarinen's role at Cranbrook was formalized: by late 1927 he had become the architect in charge, and in 1932 he was made the first President of the Academy of Art, a post he held until 1946.

When the Saarinens first moved to Cranbook, they stayed in a 1911 concrete-block farmhouse that lay close to the site of the boys' school. But life on a building site soon proved too much, and they went to live nearby with their daughter and her architect husband. In 1928 the trustees of the Cranbrook Foundation approved the idea of a new house on the campus – designed by Saarinen himself – and this was finished by September 1930, when the couple returned from their summer holiday in Finland.

BELOW The hall runs almost the full length of the entrance front, forming a buffer zone between the main living rooms and the street outside.

From the outside, Academy Group Residence No. 1, formerly known as the President's House and now as Saarinen House, is pleasant but ordinary, and perfectly in keeping with George Gough Booth's nineteenth-century Arts and Crafts ideals. It is built of brown brick with a green-tiled roof; at first glance the vertical strips of brick on the upper story evoke images of timber-framing, and those images are reinforced by leaded lights in the windows – as if Saarinen were still in thrall to figures such as Baillie Scott.

But he wasn't. Step inside Saarinen House and, no matter how improbable it may seem, you move seamlessly from Arts and Crafts to a very European Art Deco, as the earnest Ruskinian becomes a Scandinavian-American *ensemblier*. The long, dramatic living room is filled with elegant veneered furniture and dominated by a rectilinear tiled fireplace in brown and silver by local ceramicist Mary Chase Perry Stratton. This lies at right angles to an octagonal dining room, one of America's purest Art Deco interiors, with fluted chairs apparently inlaid with ebony but in reality painted in black – a device that no self-respecting Arts and Crafts cabinetmaker would countenance, and a crime that any Paris *ensemblier* would commit without a second thought. Much of the furniture was designed by Saarinen and manufactured by Tor Berglund or the New York firm of W. & J. Sloane; fabric and rugs were designed by Loja Saarinen.

The house is that total work of art that was the aim of so many Arts and Crafts architects – and yet it demonstrates how far Saarinen had come since his early days in Finland; and how elegant and restrained his European Deco was in comparison with the vulgar exuberance of American Moderne.

ABOVE Both furnishings and architecture contrive to focus the visitor's eye on the tiled fireplace at one end of the long living room. The tiles were designed by Mary Chase Perry Stratton and made at the Pewabic Pottery in Detroit.

THE ATKINS HOUSE

ALBERT GARNETT FOR PERCY ATKINS, 1936

History favors big buildings – the pyramids, St Peter's in Rome, the palace of Versailles. This is just as true of Art Deco and the 1920s and 1930s as of any other style or period. Think about the great Deco monuments: in New York, William Van Alen's 319m (1046ft) high Chrysler Building (1930) and Shreve, Lamb & Harmon's Empire State Building of the following year; Herbert J. Rowse's ventilation stations for the 1934 Mersey Tunnel in Liverpool, England, and the huge Cincinnati Union Terminal of 1933, designed by Wank and Cret. Even when it comes to homes, it is either the Deco equivalents of the stately home – the Butler House (see pages 38–41) in Des Moines, Iowa, or Burnham Beeches (see pages 26–7) in Melbourne – or the big apartment blocks and experiments in communal living, which so intrigued architects between the wars, that grab our attention.

So the ordinary Art Deco or Moderne house tends to be overlooked, neglected as not being grand enough. Yet there are thousands of such houses in suburbs all over the world: modest one- or two-story houses, often hovering between Modern and Moderne, with mandatory flat roofs, concrete or roughcast exteriors, and a hint of Deco in the minimalist decoration – a stepped-back entrance, perhaps, or a Liner Style railing on a curved balcony. Often the architect has long been forgotten, although more often there never was one – just a local builder who tried his hand at something different.

The house built by Percy Atkins on Pepper Street in Hastings – then a small town just inland from Hawke's Bay on New Zealand's North Island –

RIGHT The kitchen of the Atkins House has recently been redecorated. Indeed the present occupants have extensively restored the whole house, going to great lengths to retain period features and to introduce appropriate furniture.

LEFT The asymmetrical fireplace and the light fixture are both original to the house. The furnishings, among them the Deco mirror over the fire, were brought in more recently.

BELOW A 1920s Edison gramophone stands in the entrance hall, which still boasts an abundance of decorative wood, including elegant polished octagonal columns.

is a perfect example of this undramatic domestic Deco. Atkins was a jockey who rode regularly for a wealthy businessman named Sir Robert Kerridge, and a regular visitor to Kerridge's Art Deco holiday home at Gisborne, some 150km (90 miles) to the north. He decided he would like a Deco home of his own, and commissioned one from the established Hawke's Bay architect Albert Garnett. Like many of his contemporaries, Garnett was adept at building in any style, from Spanish Mission to English Arts and Crafts. However, there was a growing fashion for Art Deco in Hastings, dating from 1931, when the town was hit by the same earthquake that destroyed nearby Napier (see pages 96–9). Garnett had adopted the style with enthusiasm: his Carlsson Flats (1933) was one of the most confident Deco buildings in Hastings.

Based on Kerridge's in Gisborne, the Atkins House has a curious green stucco finish (then popular in the area), which simulates masonry blocks. Only one story high, it has a determined lack of symmetry: steps and a gleaming rail lead up to the front door, which is set to one side of the entrance façade under a floating curved porch. To the left there is a curved corner bay – so curved, in fact, that it conjures up memories of turrets and towers, despite the fact that it cuts off at the level of the roofline. Two flashes of color, stepped pairs of horizontal lines projecting from the façade on each side (and of unequal length), complete the picture of a building that is at once an accomplished piece of Art Deco architecture and a pleasant home.

OVERLEAF Albert Garnett moved casually between styles throughout his career in Hawke's Bay. The low, sleek lines of the Atkins House show that the architect had a particularly sure touch when it came to the Moderne.

THE BUTLER HOUSE

KRAETSCH & KRAETSCH FOR EARL BUTLER, 1934–6

I n 1937, the year after his futuristic home was completed, Earl Butler wrote: "There isn't anything in or out of the house that doesn't serve a purpose. The idea was to provide convenient facilities for pleasant outdoor living in good weather, and an interior that would meet the same requirements when the weather was inclement… We have tried to include all the things which add to the pleasure and convenience of a home without anything in the nature of a gadget."

Some might say he was being a little disingenuous. The house described in the press as "the most modern home in the world," and by the General Electric Company as the "modern show place of the nation," a home "planned for true electrical living," was packed to the rafters with gadgets. Some were advanced for their day but still utilitarian, like the thermostatically controlled heating and air-conditioning, the electric waste-disposal system,

the water softener and dishwasher, and cold-storage areas (one for meat and one for game). Then there were electric eyes that operated the doors of the three-car garage: two flashes of the headlights opened the first door, three the second, and four the third. An impressive 5800m (19,000ft) of telephone cable connected eight phones and three door phones; and there was a "portable electric broiler for steak fries in the recreation room or on the terraces." But one can't help wondering at the frosted-glass panel in the dining-room ceiling, which concealed ninety-six red, blue, and yellow bulbs, and which was controlled, as an awestruck writer in *Architectural Forum* for September 1937 pointed out, "by switches and dimmers in the pantry which permit any desired color or intensity to be obtained." And a freezer dedicated solely to providing 675 ice cubes at a time?

The Butler House was one of the most astonishing homes to be built in 1930s America. Part Le Corbusier, part Flash Gordon, it epitomizes Streamline Moderne. And it says so much about popular aspirations in the

OPPOSITE Earl Butler (left) with C.W. Appleton, GEC's vice president (center), and friend. In the Butler House, GEC executives saw a chance for a major advertising coup.

BELOW The monolithic concrete-and-steel Butler House has deservedly become the icon of the Moderne movement in American architecture.

RIGHT A gentle ramp snakes from the basement to the top of the central tower. Butler said it allowed old people "to meter their rise and descent to their physical ability."

ABOVE Earl Butler (left) and C.W. Appleton of GEC admire the view during a visit to monitor progress on site. The huge, grid-like frames holding the glass were designed specially by the Truscon Steel Co.

BELOW The second-floor living room, pictured here in September 1937, makes the most of the views over the surrounding countryside.

United States in the years after the Wall Street Crash of 1929. New technology must be harnessed for comfort and convenience; traditional notions of domestic intimacy must give way to a brighter future. When the Depression was behind them and they had emerged stronger and richer than before, the American people had a right to expect that the house of tomorrow would supply them with portable electric grills and 675-cube freezers.

As it happened, the General Electric Company, which provided most of the equipment and, in return, used Butler's home as a flagship in its advertising campaigns, called it its "house of tomorrow" – a proud reference to Norman Bel Geddes's unbuilt fantasy of 1931 (see pages 20–1). In 1934, when he bought the 4.5-hectare (11-acre) hilltop site in Des Moines, Iowa, Butler was a wealthy forty-seven-year-old real-estate manager who had spent much of the 1920s traveling around the world and planning how he would eventually settle down and build the home of his dreams. The house was realized and improved on by Earl Butler and his architect and friend George Kraetsch, of the local firm Kraetsch & Kraetsch. Butler and Kraetsch worked in an extraordinarily close partnership – so close that it is impossible to separate the two men's contributions to the design.

That design was created using 25cm (10in) exterior walls of monolithic reinforced concrete – 115 train-car loads of it – and more than 112 tonnes (110 tons) of steel. Terraces and sun decks on the roofs were in colored concrete. The ground floor, which was more like a basement, was largely taken up with services and domestic offices, including the heating and air-conditioning plants, the compressor for the refrigeration plant, the garage, and the kitchen and laundry. There was also a modest entrance hall and a large recreation and card room, with built-in bar and radio. The latter was controlled from a panel on the wall, as were recessed lighting units in the ceiling designed to provide "high-intensity glareless illumination."

The floor above contained another entrance, another hall, and the main reception rooms – a dining room, a living room of 8.25m x 5.75m (27ft x 19ft), which opened onto a railed sun deck, and a little library of 4.5m x

4.25m (15ft x 14ft) with curved walls. Over the garage there was a second kitchen and rooms for the two maids. There were four big bedrooms on the floor above, each with its own bathroom; and a sun room on the roof opened onto a big sun deck.

But by far the most curious feature of the house was the method that Butler and Kraetsch chose for moving between one floor and another. The eastern and western halves of the building were separated, from top to bottom, by a narrow, north–south structure 18m (60ft) tall, which looked rather like a giant conning tower. This housed a 90m (300ft) long ramp that pursued an elliptical spiral right from the basement to the sun room at the top. Floors led off the spiral on seven half-levels, and as a result, the floor levels in the western half of the house were 1.5m (4ft 9in) lower than those in the eastern half. The story soon got about that Butler had introduced this odd arrangement, which inevitably invites comparison with Le Corbusier's Villa Savoye (see pages 70–5), in the hope of a visit from wheelchair-bound President Roosevelt.

Time has been kind to the Butler House. After thirty years in their "house of tomorrow," the Butlers sold it to the Open Bible College in 1966, opting for a more convenient apartment in town. (Both Mr and Mrs Butler died in 1970, aged eighty-four.) Few alterations were made to the building, and when the College moved on in 1986, it was sold to an advertising agency, Kragie/Newell Advertising, which has lovingly restored and renovated it.

ABOVE Projecting balconies and terraces and stepped-back elevations make the plan of each floor of the house quite different.

GERAGH

MICHAEL SCOTT FOR HIMSELF, 1937–8

S andycove is a pleasant seaside town just south of Dublin. Drive along the seafront today and you'll see children paddling and playing on the pebble beaches, streets lined with Victorian villas, and, perched on a slight promontory looking out to sea, Sandycove's most famous building – the nineteenth-century Martello tower at the top of which stately, plump Buck Mulligan made his oblation to the gods at the beginning of James Joyce's novel *Ulysses*. But just a few steps from the Joyce Tower, and lying in its shadow, is another memorial to Irish Modernism. Michael Scott's Geragh, named after the valley in County Kerry where his father was raised, may not have been as influential as *Ulysses*, but in its own way it helped to put Irish architecture on the map.

This is no small achievement. Accounts of the architectural history of the twentieth century have little or nothing to say about Ireland. It is as though the great movements in architecture simply passed it by; and to a certain extent this is true. The years of strife leading up to political independence from Britain in 1922 were followed by further struggle and uncertainty as Ireland sought to achieve a measure of economic self-sufficiency. While this might have led to a determined break with the architecture of the past, as it did in post-revolutionary Russia, it didn't here: the need for tradition and stability was too strong and, one might argue, the power of the Roman Catholic Church too great. Landmark buildings, such as the new Catholic cathedral at Mullingar in County Westmeath (W.H. Byrne, 1930–6), tended

ABOVE Unusually, Scott's
house looks inland rather
than out to sea. This gives
some privacy from the
public path that runs past it
on the seaward side.

to be deeply conservative in style. The same was true in Protestant Ulster: Arnold Thornley's Parliament Building at Stormont (1927–32) was an incredibly reactionary piece of monumental classicism.

The new spirit in architecture was not entirely absent, however. Cinemas carried none of the baggage of the past and, since new functions seemed to call for new forms, Jazz Modern façades popped up here and there, with zigzags and stepped silhouettes – often designed by British rather than Irish architects – making their appearance all over the country in the 1930s. Public and commercial buildings also started, very slowly, to exhibit Modernist tendencies: one thinks immediately of Desmond FitzGerald's magnificent Dublin Airport Terminal of 1936–40. But Modern or Moderne houses were a rarity. And that makes Michael Scott's Geragh something very special.

Like many architects, Scott (1905–88) had started out determined to be a painter, but he was persuaded by his father to train as an architect. He also took up acting as a young man, and in 1927 starred in the Broadway production of Sean O'Casey's play *The Plough and the Stars*. In 1931 Scott set up in practice in Dublin with Norman Good, and over the next seven years the partnership designed public buildings, cinemas, and offices in a blocky, horizontal De Stijl manner.

But Scott's interest in Modernism was growing. In 1937 he became President of the Architectural Association of Ireland, and was instrumental in attracting guest lecturers such as Walter Gropius, who spoke on "The International Trend of Modern Architecture"; and Erich Mendelsohn, who told the Irish architectural establishment all about "Rebuilding the World."

ABOVE One of Geragh's porthole windows. Scott's use of nautical imagery not only reflects a phase of Modernism in the early 1930s, but also is apt for a seaside home.

BELOW The bow windows, which do so much to define the distinctive exterior of the house, also have a considerable impact on the interiors, as this view of the main living room shows.

During his presidency of the AAI, from 1937 to 1938, Scott broke up with Good, started his own practice, and built Geragh. Several years earlier he had bought the site, an old quarry with literature's famous Martello tower on one side and the Forty Foot, a nineteenth-century stone fortification and male bathing area, on the other, using an inheritance of more than £5000 that his wife Patricia had recently received. This money also allowed the Scotts, who were never particularly well off, to build the house after the architect's father had turned down his original suggestion that he might like the place as a seaside retreat.

Scott would later claim that Geragh was designed at a single sitting. "I started one morning at eight o'clock and by four o'clock the following morning had finished the initial sketch plans," he said: "I was a quick boy in my day." There may be a germ of truth in the story: the site had been sold to him on the understanding that he build a house on it within three years, a condition that he promptly forgot until a letter arrived to remind him of his obligations, at which point he sat down and began work. Nevertheless, Geragh had its roots in a house that Scott had designed for Arthur Shields back in 1933, when he was in partnership with Good. Preliminary sketches for the Shields house, which seems never to have gone beyond the drawing board, show a cubistic and rather unexciting entrance elevation; but the garden front is dominated by a huge, curving bay that projects out from the main body of the house and contains the living room on the ground floor and the master bedroom above.

This semi-circular curve, the Liner Style bow, which occurs so often in both early Modern-movement architecture and Streamline Moderne (and which can be seen in buildings as far removed as Mendelsohn and Chermayeff's De La Warr Pavilion and Jacobus Oud's Kiefhoek housing estate – see pages 82–5), is the feature that immediately draws the eye towards Geragh. There is a public footpath around the promontory on the seaward side, so the house faces inland rather than out to sea, and it feels like a very private place, tucked beneath the sheer walls of the old quarry and turning its back on the beaches and the holidaymakers who have long flocked to Sandycove. A cubistic set of blocks, balconies, and terraces fits close in to the quarry face, and Scott attached to them, not a single bow but a stepped-back series of curves on three levels. The lowest was simply a terrace, a railed sun deck that projected over the *pilotis* that originally supported the entire house but were later filled in to provide extra rooms. Set well back from the edge of the terrace was the second bow – the main living room, which was defined by a curve of high windows, with another, smaller sun deck above them, and yet another bow set back from that.

Discussing this distinctive arrangement of curves, Scott recalled that he designed Geragh as a series of descending circles, each wider than the previous one. "It's my tribute to the tower and to James Joyce," he said. It is satisfying to think that the more discerning visitor who comes to Sandycove to pay tribute to Joyce and his tower will pause, however briefly, to pay another tribute – to Michael Scott and to Geragh, one of Ireland's finest twentieth-century houses.

PAVILIONED IN SPLENDOR

One night in the spring of 1925 the Eiffel Tower was suddenly turned into a beacon of Art Deco, as some 200,000 colored electric light bulbs covered the entire structure in a dazzling display of curves, concentric circles, and blazing stars. Paris was celebrating the Exposition Internationale des Arts Décoratifs et Industriels Modernes, the exhibition that forty years later would give its name to Art Deco. The idea for the Exposition had been raised before World War I, when the success of the Deutscher Werkbund and Germany's reform of the relationship between design and industry had focused French reformers on the need to catch up with their traditional rivals. In 1912 a committee was appointed to organize the Exposition, which was to take place in 1915. In the event, the war and other reasons delayed it for ten years.

Located in the center of Paris, the site straddled the River Seine. The foreign pavilions were on the Right Bank, and of these, the

RIGHT Builders at work on the Porte d'Orsay, one of twelve entrances to the Exposition. The steel structure was designed by Louis Boileau and had a semi-abstract mural by Louis Voguet.

46

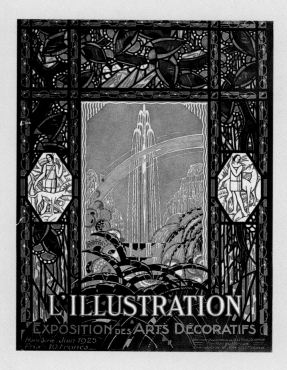

principal exhibitors were Belgium, Japan, Italy, and Britain. Germany, still in purdah after the war, was not invited until the last moment, when it was too late for it to take part. The USA decided that the organizers' aims were beyond the abilities of its contemporary designers. At the outset the organizers had declared that works submitted to the Exposition "must show new inspiration and real originality." The Americans needn't have worried too much, since ideas of what constituted new inspiration and originality varied wildly.

Louis Süe and André Mare, the *ensembliers* who had founded La Compagnie des Arts Français in 1919 (see pages 136–7), had an interesting domed pavilion, the Musée d'Art Contemporain. Their own contribution to *l'art contemporain*, however, included a set of giltwood furniture that would have been more at home in the 1820s than in the 1920s. And the sinuous, foliate forms that filled Victor Horta's Belgian Pavilion provided evidence that Art Nouveau was still alive and well in Belgium, if nowhere else. The British Pavilion designed by Easton and Robertson was not so much conservative as downright odd. It was faintly Moorish, with a tall glass cupola topped by a weathervane in the shape of a sailing ship.

Here and there were signs of genuine inspiration and originality. The Polish Pavilion of

Josef Czajkowski contained some chunky cubist furniture. Robert Mallet-Stevens's Pavillon du Tourisme drew praise from the Russian architect Konstantin Melnikov, who extolled his refusal to succumb to "dazzling Parisian chic." And the dynamic interplay of line and mass in Melnikov's own Soviet Pavilion reminded Parisians that the orthodoxies overturned by the Russian Revolution extended far beyond politics.

Among native exhibits, the Ambassade Française, or French Embassy, designed under the supervision of Henri Rapin and Pierre Selmersheim, was furnished by a collaborative network of designers and artists under the auspices of the French government and the Société des Artistes Décorateurs, which had been founded in 1901. This consisted of two linked wings containing twenty-four model rooms. One wing housed the offices and ambassadorial reception areas, the other the ambassador's living rooms. There was a library and a smoking room in each wing: Pierre Chareau designed one of the libraries, and Jean Dunand one of the *fumoirs*. The second *fumoir* was a bright, angular composition by Francis Jourdain, with primrose-yellow walls and black furniture. The tension between traditional and progressive ideas was exemplified by Robert Mallet-Stevens's stark, Modernist entrance hall

LEFT Like many art journals throughout Europe, the magazine *L'Illustration* issued a special edition dedicated to the Exposition. The cover is based on a stained-glass panel by Jeannin Gaetan.

BELOW Studio shown by the *ensemblier* Lucie Renaudot, with furniture of macassar ebony by Dumas, vases by Jean Dunand, and sculpture by Parayre. In the 1930s Renaudot would design cabins for various liners, including the *Normandie*.

and Rapin and Selmersheim's *grand salon*, opulent, but deeply conservative and filled with rich browns and pale beiges.

The exhibition site was to be cleared as soon as the Exposition closed in October, so commercial architects were free to indulge their imaginations. As a result, the pavilions of the *ensembliers* and the ateliers of the big department stores were unrestrained. Galeries Lafayette's La Maîtrise, by Hiriart, Tribout, and Beau, had an entrance formed by a massive sunburst; Printemps' Primavera Pavilion (by Sauvage and Vybo) looked like a Mayan temple in a silent movie; and the Pomone Pavilion of Au Bon Marché, by Louis Boileau, was a magical piece of High Deco with stepped wings, an octagonal central section, and a huge glass panel of curves and zigzags. The couturier Paul Poiret's offering consisted of three barges moored beneath the Pont Alexandre III, which connected the two halves of the Exposition. *Délices* was a high-class restaurant, and *Orgues* was a floating fashion show, displaying Poiret's latest collection against a backdrop of painted Jazz Age hangings by Raoul Dufy. *Amours*, which was decked out by Poiret's Atelier Martine, contained furniture and decoration for a modern apartment, in a striking combination of emerald greens and scarlets and with nods in the direction of the Ballets Russes, the Viennese Secession, and African exoticism.

But the star of the show was the Hôtel du Collectionneur, which housed a group of interiors from the master cabinetmaker and *ensemblier* Jacques-Emile Ruhlmann. Designed by Pierre Patout, it was more restrained than the pavilions of Au Bon Marché and Galeries Lafayette. Instead of sunbursts and zigzags, Patout produced a controlled façade in which the main block stepped back from two columned wings in a series of steps. External decoration was limited to a splendid iron gate by Edgar Brandt, and Joseph Bernard's frieze of stylized, rather classical figures who danced around the upper section of a curving bow window that dominated the main front and formed the exterior expression of the oval *grand salon*, which stood at the pavilion's center. *A la gloire de Jean Goujon*, a group made by Alfred-Auguste Janniot in homage to the Renaissance French sculptor, stood in front of the building, suggesting that Ruhlmann and his craftsmen were heirs to a great tradition rather than progressives consciously breaking with the past.

But it wasn't the architecture that drew visitors in their hundreds of thousands to the Hôtel du Collectionneur. The pavilion was laid out in the form of a grand mansion, with salon, dining room, bedroom, study, and boudoir. These interiors were unashamedly opulent – so much so that even the most libertarian and hedonistic visitor was amazed, and perhaps a little shocked. The boudoir was a harmony of green and gold, with white-marble fireplace and silk-covered furniture; the bedroom was decorated in pinks and greys, hung with ivory damask, and furnished with ebony and ivory commode and fur-covered bed, bedside tables, and wing chair. The oval salon was hung with patterned silk; its curtains were light-grey silk; and the whole room was lit by a massive crystal chandelier and silver-bronze lamps festooned with clusters of crystal pearls. A

BELOW Fountain in the Cour des Métiers designed by René Lalique and Marc Ducluzeaud. A major presence at the Exposition, Lalique had his own pavilion and collaborated on important installations in several others.

Exposition des Arts Décoratifs
PAVILLON DE GRANDE-BRETAGNE

macassar-ebony grand piano by Gaveau and a lacquer cabinet by Jean Dunand vied with chairs covered in Aubusson tapestry.

Years after the Exposition, Ruhlmann was still defending his rich interiors and the rich clients who paid for them. "New creations have never been made for the middle classes," he said. "They have always been made at the request of an élite which unsparingly gives artists the time and money needed for laborious research and perfect execution." This was a lesson that William Morris had learned in the nineteenth century.

But the Hôtel du Collectionneur was pushing against the spirit of the age, as was the whole High Deco movement epitomized by Ruhlmann and his friends. Tucked in a corner of the exhibition site was a strange, austere building with a tree growing up through its roof. It was hidden on the edge of the complex because it embarrassed the authorities. But its influence would spread until it dominated Western architecture. It was the Pavillon de l'Esprit Nouveau of Le Corbusier.

MACHINES
FOR LIVING IN

It is sometimes said that Art Deco's most important function was to mediate between past and future; between the traditional – and hence respectable – forms of the eighteenth and nineteenth centuries and the new design vocabulary that was being created out of Modernism in the first three or four decades of the twentieth. According to this version of events, as *ensembliers* like Jacques-Emile Ruhlmann or Eileen Gray moved from macassar ebony to chrome and steel, they took their clients with them. When a designer like Robert Mallet-Stevens served up architecture that blended Russian Constructivism with Deco detail, the public found it more acceptable than an undiluted version.

To suggest that this was a deliberate move would perhaps be to claim too much for a style that was essentially frivolous, hedonistic, and supremely uncerebral; looking for a serious intellectual purpose in Art Deco is an enterprise doomed to failure. But it is nevertheless true that Deco forged relationships with the weightier architectural movements that were emerging all around it, borrowing from them and, in the process, helping to make them more acceptable to the public. If this happened more by accident than by design, because Jazz Modern had no substance of its own, that still doesn't make the basic premise false.

And there was an overlap, at times quite considerable, between Art Deco and those other styles and movements. One doesn't have to strain very hard to see links between Art Deco and the Art Nouveau buildings of Charles Rennie

Mackintosh, such as the reading room at his Glasgow School of Art (1907–9) or the Willow Tea Rooms (1902–4) in the same city; or the output of the Deutscher Werkbund or De Stijl.

However, Art Deco didn't only borrow from its precursors. It took from its contemporaries as well, when these met its needs. And many of its designers moved in the same artistic circles as those non-Deco contemporaries. One has only to think of the appearance of Le Corbusier's Pavillon de l'Esprit Nouveau at the 1925 Exposition in Paris or the splendid sight of a terrace of three houses at Boulogne-sur-Mer, France: one by the Deutscher Werkbund architect Theodor Fischer; the second by Robert Mallet-Stevens, probably Deco's greatest architect; and the third by Le Corbusier himself.

In domestic architecture, the line between Art Deco and Modernism was especially blurred. As we have seen, Deco was basically a public style: it thrived in the high-rise office blocks of Manhattan, the department stores of Paris and London, and the cinemas that sprang up in

PREVIOUS PAGE Villa Savoye, Poissy, France, by Le Corbusier, 1928–31.

ABOVE A row of houses in Boulogne-sur-Mer, France. The house on the left is by Robert Mallet-Stevens; the one in the middle by Le Corbusier; and the one on the right by Theodor Fischer, a founding member of the Deutscher Werkbund.

LEFT A detail of Gerrit Rietveld's Schröder House. The De Stijl movement was ideologically motivated, but its fascination with primary colors and plain surfaces had an impact on the less earnest approach of Art Deco architects.

thousands of provincial cities and towns all over the world in the 1920s and 1930s. When Deco turned to homes, it happily stole from the vocabulary of Modernism – or, to put it more politely, it managed to reinterpret key Modern movement themes. It took the house as "a machine for living in," in Le Corbusier's legendary phrase, and it streamlined the machine.

In their different ways, the buildings in this chapter are all machines for living in. They range in date from Robert van't Hoff's 1915 Villa Henny, an early icon of the Dutch De Stijl movement, to Le Corbusier's even more iconic Villa Savoye in Paris (1928–31); taking in on the way Gerrit Rietveld's Schröder House in Utrecht, another classic of De Stijl; Peter Behrens's New Ways, England's first modern house; Richard Neutra's Lovell House in Los Angeles, an experiment in healthy living; and E.1027, Eileen Gray's wonderful seaside retreat at Roquebrune-Cap Martin, France. Every one of these houses is an experiment of sorts, an attempt to discover an architecture that would allow more efficient, more congenial living.

BELOW Le Corbusier's famous and iconic Pavillon de l'Esprit Nouveau, a prototype for mass-produced living units, was tucked out of sight by the bemused organizers of the 1925 Paris Exposition.

Le Corbusier & P. Jeanneret
Architectes

Exposition des Arts Décoratifs
Pavillon de l'Esprit Nouveau

192
AN
PARIS

VILLA HENNY

ROBERT VAN'T HOFF, 1915–19

Concrete has a long and honorable history as a building material, a history that stretches back to the great engineering works of the ancient Romans and beyond. As far as domestic architecture is concerned, by the nineteenth century at least one English country house, the Italianate Down Hall in Essex (C.R. Cockerell, 1871–3), had walls of poured and shuttered concrete; and iron-reinforced concrete was used by the French builder François Coignet in the construction of his own house in Paris in 1862.

By the early years of the twentieth century, concrete was being used all over the place: in slab form, in Frank Lloyd Wright's D.D. Martin House at Buffalo, New York, for example; as exposed walling, in Bernard Maybeck's classic First Church of Christ Scientist in Berkeley, California (1910); and with remarkable effect as a sculptural and organic material in Antoni Gaudí's apartment buildings, such as the extraordinary Casa Milá in Barcelona

BELOW With its strong rectilinear design and the use of different colors to emphasize particular elements, the experimental Villa Henny looks forward to De Stijl.

(1905–10). No wonder that by 1900 even the conservative British architectural establishment could accept that, as Richard Norman Shaw told W.R. Lethaby, "Reinforced concrete ought to do a lot for us."

But the point about all these examples, with the possible exception of Wright, is that no one really imagined that concrete might create its own aesthetic, its own unique design vocabulary. It "ought to do a lot for us" by offering cheaply molded applied ornament, or concrete frames to clad in traditional brick or stone.

That is what makes so special the villa that Robert van't Hoff built at Huis-ter-Heide, near Utrecht, in the Netherlands, during and immediately after World War I. It did create its own aesthetic; and in so doing, it opened the door to a new world of structural opportunities for those architects who built houses and who chose to turn their back on the past.

Van't Hoff (1887–1979) was born in Rotterdam and studied architecture in England, first at the Birmingham School of Art (1906–11), where staff were still heavily influenced by William Morris and the Arts and Crafts movement; and then, from 1911 to 1914, at the Architectural Association in London. In 1913 his father gave him a copy of the Ernst Wasmuth portfolio of Wright's *Studies and Executed Buildings*, which contained the Concrete House that Wright had originally published in the *Ladies' Home Journal*. So impressed was van't Hoff that he left London in June 1913 and rushed to the United States, where he sought out Wright and spent more than a year studying contemporary American architecture.

In July 1914, just before the outbreak of war, he returned to the Netherlands. He built a summer house named Verloop at Huis-ter-Heide; and then, around 1915, he designed the concrete-framed Villa Henny, one of the first Modernist houses of the twentieth century. The building type would be taken up by architects across Europe – flat, angular, devoid of external ornament, with projecting eaves and canopies, horizontal grids of window and an uncompromising belief in the universality of contemporary architecture. Houses would never be the same again.

ABOVE Almost half of the ground floor was taken up with this big south-facing living and dining room, which had a study, kitchen, pantry, bathroom, and hall packed in behind it.

LEFT Villa Henny under construction. Van't Hoff was profoundly influenced by Frank Lloyd Wright's prairie houses of the turn of the century, and by the American architect's experiments with concrete.

THE SCHRÖDER HOUSE

GERRIT RIETVELD FOR AND WITH TRUUS SCHRÖDER-SCHRÄDER, 1924

<small>ABOVE</small> Gerrit Rietveld (center) pictured in about 1926, with the Dutch designer Mart Stam (left) and Russian Constructivist El Lissitzky. The latter worked with van Doesburg and formed an important link between the European avant-garde and post-Revolutionary Russia.

The Schröder House is a wonderfully peculiar building. Standing at the end of an ordinary row of houses on Prins Hendriklaan in Utrecht, the Netherlands, it displays a weird combination of plane surfaces, bright colors, and overlapping angles that confounds even our advanced twenty-first-century ideas of what a dwelling place should be. As an attempt to redefine the house, and to translate some complex aesthetic theories into brick, wood, and concrete, it has few rivals.

The theories were those that underpinned De Stijl, the movement with which the architect of the Schröder House, Gerrit Rietveld (1888–1964), became involved in 1919. Rietveld was the son of a Utrecht cabinetmaker who followed his father's profession, running his own workshop and designing furniture that was heavily influenced by Frank Lloyd Wright. Robert van't Hoff commissioned work from him for his Huis-ter-Heide projects (see pages 54–5). And through van't Hoff, Rietveld became a member of De Stijl, the Leiden-based group that included J.J.P. Oud, Piet Mondrian, Jan Wils, and Theo van Doesburg. Influenced by Mondrian's Neoplasticism, which sought to reduce volume to plane surface and propounded an almost mystical belief in the power of art to express the essential harmony of the universe, De Stijl was intent on sweeping away all vestiges of the past. As van Doesburg wrote in 1921, in the magazine that he edited and that gave the movement its name, the old Europe was dying. "We look on calmly…," he said, "we would not want to help. We do not wish to prolong the life of this old prostitute. A new Europe has already begun to grow within us."

By 1924, when work began on the designs for the Schröder House, Rietveld was already famous in avant-garde circles for his furniture, and in particular for the Red/Blue Chair, which he had been developing over the past six years. This was a wooden armchair in which a series of horizontal and vertical rectilinear planes were made to overlap where they intersected so that they broke through the boundary between the volume of the chair and the space surrounding it. When the chair was originally designed, in 1918, its plane surfaces were left unpainted, but these were later painted in black and the primary colors – red, blue, and yellow – which were favored by De Stijl for their purity and simplicity and which gave the piece its name. In 1919 Rietveld created an equally iconic sideboard, in which interlocking elements – again using horizontal and vertical planes – combine with the deliberately conspicuous spaces between them to disrupt the idea of a fixed volume. Four

years later he produced his Berlin Chair, an asymmetric piece in black, white, and two shades of grey, which comes close to being an abstract composition rather than a piece of furniture.

Rietveld had also begun to establish himself as an interior designer, having carried out commissions in Rotterdam, Katwijk, and Amsterdam. He also harbored an ambition to be an architect, despite his total lack of formal training. (In 1926 El Lissitzky remarked admiringly that, although with the Schröder House Rietveld had become "a foremost leader of the contemporary art of housing," he was a carpenter rather than an architect, and "not able routinely to draw out a plan.")

It was his compatriot Truus Schröder-Schräder who gave Rietveld the chance to try his hand as an architect. The pharmacist turned interior designer already knew his work because she had commissioned him to redecorate her house at 135 Biltstraat, Utrecht, in 1921. So when Schröder-Schräder's husband died in 1924 and she decided that she and her three children should move to a smaller, less expensive house, she turned to Rietveld to help her design it. The site they chose, on Prins Hendriklaan, was hardly prepossessing. Rietveld later remembered it as a forlorn piece of no-man's-land, overrun with weeds and edged with a crumbling wall. "And we said, 'Yes, this is just right, let's build it here.' And we took this plot of ground and made it into a place with a reality of its own."

ABOVE The Schröder House, also known as the Rietveld-Schröder House. "We took this plot of ground and made it into a place with a reality of its own."

BELOW In a photograph dating from the 1950s, Rietveld uses a model to demonstrate the construction of one of his house designs.

ABOVE The big second-floor sitting room to the left, with the children's bedrooms on the right. A flexible layout is achieved by the use of sliding wall partitions; these are open here, but they can be closed to divide the area and give privacy. A version of Rietveld's Red/Blue Chair is on the left.

So they did, turning a Mondrian painting or the Red/Blue Chair into a building. "We didn't avoid older styles because they were ugly, or because we couldn't reproduce them," said Rietveld, "but because our own times demanded their own form." He used the collective pronoun advisedly: Schröder-Schräder played an active role in the design of the house, and enjoyed it so much that she joined De Stijl herself in 1925 and collaborated with Rietveld in 1926 on a house in Amsterdam for her sister An Harrenstein and An's husband. She and Rietveld also designed a glass radio case in 1925.

What was so revolutionary about the Schröder House? Certainly not the construction itself, which, contrary to De Stijl's principles, made use not of reinforced concrete but of traditional brick for the walls and wood for the ceilings and roof. Projecting supports were carried on iron beams. But that was where tradition ended. Theo van Doesburg wrote in "Towards a Plastic Architecture" (*De Stijl* VI, 1924) that "the new architecture has broken through the wall and in so doing has completely eliminated the separation of inside and out... The new architecture is anti-cubic, that is to say, it does not try to freeze the different functional space cells in one closed cube."

This is exactly what Rietveld and Schröder-Schräder achieved: the box is broken in a way that even Frank Lloyd Wright never imagined. The brickwork of the house is painted white to disguise its texture and emphasize the plane surfaces, which, like the intersections of elements on the Red/Blue Chair, refuse to be confined within the volume of the building, blurring the boundaries between the structure and its environment. Iron girders and sections are painted red, yellow, black, and white, dramatizing the vertical and horizontal, and activating the assemblage.

The interior spaces are just as dynamic, on the upper story at least. The ground floor, occupied by a studio, study, kitchen, hallway, and staircase, is a series of fixed spaces – the result of structural considerations. But the floor above, which contains the living room, Schröder-Schräder's bedroom and bathroom, and her children's bedrooms, is much more transient, since the internal walls are no more than sliding partitions that can be opened and rearranged at will – the first occasion on which a house adopted such a flexible room plan. Rietveld and his client also went to great lengths to blur the distinction between exterior surface and interior space, using the same color scheme for both, and laying black, grey, and red felt to cover the wooden floors and produce a sense of homogeneity with the vertical planes.

As van Doesburg wrote in "Towards a Plastic Architecture," "height, width, depth, and time approach a totally new plastic expansion in open spaces." Or to put it more succinctly, the Schröder House floats.

BELOW The Schröder House by night. Facing us and looking out onto Prins Hendriklaan are a ground-floor studio and, above, the bedroom of Truus Schröder-Schräder's daughters. The window of the second-floor sitting room can just be seen on the right.

NEW WAYS

PETER BEHRENS FOR W.J. BASSETT-LOWKE, 1924–5

In 1940, in his Modernist manifesto *An Introduction to Modern Architecture*, J.M. Richards described New Ways as "the first modern building in England." And what a building it is, still with the power to delight and surprise us three-quarters of a century after it was built.

That sense of wonder was even more acute in 1924. It began with one's first glimpse of the entrance façade. From a pleasant but undistinguished suburban road on the outskirts of Northampton, ultramarine-blue garden gates opened onto a flagstone path that was lit by little pylon-shaped lamps and led down to a sunken garden. There the house stood (and still stands), supremely un-English and utterly beautiful. The severity of plain, ivory-white walls – not concrete, but cement render over rough bricks – is relieved by the tall, V-shaped window that lights the staircase (see montage on page 62). This feature, which was destined to crop up with great frequency in English Modernism, cuts the façade in two. It rises from a concrete canopy with spiky little ornaments at each corner and a center decorated with five stubby concrete

BELOW In 1926 the *Architectural Review* printed this picture of New Ways with a caption describing it as "an amusing photograph which emphasizes the tremendous clash of contrast between the two types of house."

projections that point down to double doors, again of ultramarine blue. The V-window goes up to the eaves, where odd little black concrete crestings sprout from the flat, bitumenized roof. Metal casements flank the doors, but this is the only window on the upper story of the façade, and the blind ivory walls to either side force us to focus our attention on it, while at the same time it evokes southern European or perhaps even north African architecture. We have the sense that New Ways goes to great lengths to keep out the hot sun; and even though this problem would be of little concern to suburban householders in Northamptonshire, here the treatment nevertheless feels wholly appropriate.

The garden front is less Jazz Modern, more open, and so more restful. It also boasts concrete crestings on the roof, but the center is taken up by a little ground-floor loggia, which opens out of the centrally placed dining room; and, on the floor above, by a recessed verandah, which gives onto a boudoir flanked by the two main bedrooms, both of which have access to this balcony.

In 1924 there was no British architect capable of designing a Modernist tour de force like New Ways; and with the possible exceptions of E. Maxwell Fry and Oliver Hill, there wouldn't be for another twenty-five years. The architect was the German Peter Behrens (1868–1940), the recently appointed director of the School of Architecture at the Akademie der bildenden Künste in Vienna. Behrens, who had taught Le Corbusier, Gropius, and Mies van der Rohe, had been one of the pioneers of industrial design, creating a corporate image for the German electrical company AEG as early as 1907, when an integrated approach to product design, graphic art, and the architecture of the workplace was extremely rare. His buildings, which tended towards a severe and monumental functionalism, included the AEG turbine factory at Moabit in Berlin, Germany's first glass-and-steel structure (1908–9); the German Embassy in St Petersburg (1911–12); and the almost classical Cuno House at Eppenhausen on the edge of Germany's Ruhr conurbation (1910).

Behrens's client, Wenman Joseph Bassett-Lowke, was a likeable character with an abiding interest in unconventional architecture. After working in his family engineering firm in Northampton, Bassett-Lowke set up a mail-order business producing scale models of British steam engines. Bassett-Lowke Ltd thrived, and by the early 1920s its proprietor had shops in London, Manchester, and Edinburgh, and was making not only toys but also highly detailed exhibition models that were shown in boardrooms and museums all over the world. As the *Daily Mail* reported, his customers "ranged from small boys to oriental princes, from millionaires to kings."

In March 1917 Bassett-Lowke married Florence Jane Jones, daughter of another Northampton industrialist, and the couple moved into 78 Derngate, a Georgian terraced house in the center of town that Bassett-Lowke's father had bought the previous year for £250. The house was modernized by Alexander Ellis Anderson, a local architect with a distinctive style; but after a chance meeting with a Glaswegian friend who was full of enthusiasm for the work of Charles Rennie Mackintosh, Bassett-Lowke asked Mackintosh to redesign the whole of the interior, and also gave him several minor commissions, including work on his country retreat, Candida Cottage.

After World War I the toy manufacturer bought a plot measuring 90m x 180m (300ft x 600ft) on the edge of Northampton, intending to ask

ABOVE A portrait of Peter Behrens painted by Max Liebermann in 1913. The architect's design for New Ways shocked the British public – a reaction that, one suspects, was not altogether unwelcome to his client.

THE FOUNDATIONS OF
THE EMPIRE ARE
IN THE HOMES
OF THE PEOPLE
KING GEORGE V.

Christmas 1940

WITH THE SEASON'S GREETINGS FROM
MR. & MRS. BASSETT-LOWKE, NEW WAYS, NORTHAMPTON

NEW WAYS

ABOVE For their Christmas card in 1940 the Bassett-Lowkes chose a montage of exterior and interior scenes from New Ways. The couple sit at a tea table just left of the center of the picture, below the V-shaped window.

Mackintosh to design a house for him on the site. This was in 1924, however; and by then the Scotsman was living in France. "I could not find any other architect with modern ideas in England," Bassett-Lowke later recalled; "and when looking through a German publication called *Werkbund Jahrbuch* of 1913 I saw some work by Professor Peter Behrens which I thought was very simple, straightforward, and modern in its atmosphere." An impulsive man, the manufacturer obtained Behrens's address from the German Consulate and, after some cursory negotiations, commissioned him to build New Ways. He did, however, insist that the hall of 78 Derngate was to be reproduced as the study of the new house, which looked out over the front garden. His idea was that the room, with its primrose-yellow walls and stenciled geometrical frieze in orange, grey, blue, red, and yellow, would be suitable for a nursery, should the occasion arise. Sadly, it never did.

There were other conditions, too. The lounge should be large enough for dancing, while the dining room should be quite small, since it was to be a functional space reserved purely for eating. A Fabian socialist – George Bernard Shaw was a friend and a regular visitor to New Ways – Bassett-Lowke insisted that his maids must have their own sitting room and that their sleeping quarters should have hot and cold running water. Electricity in every room was essential, as was central heating, although Bassett-Lowke wanted a coal fire in the living room "on account of its sentimental value and human appeal." He personally designed the kitchen, the bedrooms, and their adjacent dressing-bathrooms, and his overall contribution was significant enough for the house to be described in the architectural press in 1928 as having been designed by "Professor Dr. P. Behrens and W.J. Bassett-Lowke."

But credit for the remarkable exteriors goes to Behrens alone; and one suspects that the architecture of the interior is likewise all his, although his client made decisions on the upstairs furnishings and color schemes. Behrens created a beautiful design for the floor of the entrance hall, made up of black, white, and grey tiles in different sizes – almost like a monochrome Mondrian, and complemented perfectly by enameled grey doors, a blue carpet, and primrose-yellow walls. To judge from photographs taken at the time, this was one of the most successful rooms in the house. It was closely followed by the living room, which had glazed wall panels to either side of the fireplace that had been made in Berlin but were reminiscent of stained glass by Mackintosh or Frank Lloyd Wright. And Bassett-Lowke himself had a fine – and very modern – eye for decoration. The living-room furniture was of dark oak and made by local craftsmen; the carpet, however, was a heady composition in striking red, blue, yellow, and green that he had bought from Atelier Primavera at the Le Printemps department store in Paris (see pages 136–7); the master bedroom was a striking combination of cerise and blue, with purple curtains and furniture that was painted grey; and the guest room had light oak furniture, a bright green carpet, walls of silver and white stripes, and curtains patterned in blue, red, and orange.

New Ways burst onto the British architectural scene like a bombshell. People were aware of European experiments in avant-garde housing design; but, on the whole, they thought that Europe was where they should stay. "Doubts have been expressed as to the suitability of the type to English conditions and thought," noted the *Architectural Review*, which also printed a photograph of the house sandwiched between its neighbors, two extremely conventional Stockbroker Tudor villas. In fact, the magazine was not really sure what to make of Behrens's and Bassett-Lowke's creation, and it contented itself with being patronizing. New Ways was "intended not only to be but to look a modern house." A pendant light in the Mackintosh study was, like the photograph, "amusing"; the exterior was "somewhat bizarre"; and the house as a whole was "most cosmopolitan" and "a gay example of a personal taste."

A less conservative reaction came from the young architect Frederick McManus, personal assistant to Thomas S. Tait. He said that New Ways "acted as the catalyst for the Silver End houses" (see pages 90–1) with which Tait was to make his name, and that the sight of the building "released me from the traditional forms in which I had been so long immersed."

In 1948, twenty-three years after New Ways was completed, the local press gave Bassett-Lowke his greatest accolade. Commending his "prodding, persuasive interest in good design as an increasing part of everyday living," the *Chronicle & Echo* declared him to be "an example of the tolerance that wide vision and sympathies can give." If there had been more patrons with his vision, the architectural history of Britain in the twentieth century would have been very different indeed.

BELOW Another Christmas card commissioned by the Bassett-Lowkes, this one from 1935. Ernest Noble's drawing shows Bassett-Lowke perched on the wing of an airplane holding a movie camera, with New Ways standing on the quay beneath him.

THE SEASON'S GREETINGS FROM EVERY ANGLE AND "NEW WAYS" NORTHAMPTON.

THE LOVELL HOUSE

RICHARD NEUTRA FOR DR. PHILIP LOVELL, 1927–9

r. Philip Lovell was a young man of advanced views. A weekend columnist for the *Los Angeles Times*, he was a tireless advocate of the virtues of a diet containing plenty of fruit and vegetables, the importance of taking regular and frequent exercise, and the health-giving properties of the open-air life. None of this is revolutionary today, but in the 1920s it was quite daring and decidedly eccentric: the medical establishment was of the opinion that sunshine had a stupefying effect on the mind, and too much exercise was thought to be physically damaging and morally suspect.

Fortunately for us, Lovell's eccentricities extended to architecture. In 1925 he asked Frank Lloyd Wright's erstwhile assistant Rudolph Schindler to design a house for him at Newport Beach, Los Angeles. Schindler was a kindred spirit: his family followed a similarly "advanced" lifestyle, living on simple meals of fruit and vegetables and wearing loose-fitting, "rational" clothing. The result of the collaboration was the Lovell Beach House, one of America's greatest contributions to the Modern movement and arguably Schindler's finest work. Uncompromisingly modern and rectilinear, the Beach House is based on the idea of a duplex living room with balcony and bedrooms raised on five huge frames of reinforced concrete and cantilevered into the main space. Schindler was hurt by the mixed reception given to the house: it was too unconventional for the old guard but not functional enough to merit the approval of the avant-garde, and it was excluded from the important International Style exhibition held at the Museum of Modern Art in New York in 1932. This was unfair, as Schindler (and others) have pointed out: the five frames that support the upper story provide a covered space for open-air living, raise the main building above the public beach, and create a skeletal frame that is flexible enough to withstand earthquakes.

Lovell was delighted with the Beach House, and he asked Schindler to design another holiday retreat for him: a cabin in the mountains. But in 1927, the year after the Beach House was completed, he decided that he wanted an altogether grander residence in Los Angeles, on a precipitous and difficult site that he had acquired in Griffith Park, between Hollywood and the San Fernando Valley. This time the job didn't go to Schindler. It went to his friend and partner, Richard Neutra (1892–1970).

OPPOSITE The Lovell House, named for Los Angeles doctor Philip Lovell, was also known as the Demonstration Health House, because Lovell intended it as an advertisement for his theories on what constituted healthy living.

ABOVE Interest in the Lovell House was so great that when Philip Lovell invited the public to tour the house, 15,000 people took up his offer. Its fame spread, and it was one of the first modern buildings in Los Angeles to achieve recognition in Europe.

LEFT Neutra in later life, consulting with members of his staff. Well versed in the practical side of construction, the architect was apparently able to erect the steel frame of the Lovell House in only forty hours.

Neutra had a pedigree that read like a who's who of modernist design. Born in Vienna, he knew Adolf Loos in the years before World War I, and was profoundly influenced by the latter's functionalist approach to building and, in particular, by his seminal 1908 lecture on "Ornament and Crime" in which he declared that "the evolution of culture marches with the elimination of ornament from useful objects." Loos was fascinated with American architecture – Neutra later said the older man was most impressed by the people, who were "all caught up in the same process of upheaval, and all … converted to a new kind of realism, free from the historic prejudices which had thickened and poisoned their blood." Neutra never forgot Loos's enthusiasm for the United States; and after a spell in Berlin in the early 1920s, where he collaborated with Erich Mendelsohn, he emigrated to America in 1923. He traveled to Chicago to seek out his hero, the sick and impoverished Louis Sullivan. Neutra was one of the very few mourners to follow Sullivan's coffin when the old man died in April 1924. Another was Frank Lloyd Wright, with whom Neutra spent three months at the Taliesin Community in Wisconsin before arriving in Los Angeles, where he set up a practice in the office of Schindler, an old acquaintance from pre-war Vienna.

Although Neutra and his wife were living in the Schindler House on King's Road in West Hollywood, the two men were barely on speaking terms by 1927. Schindler had not forgiven the fact that a joint design they had submitted for the League of Nations competition was published in Europe by Neutra's family – with Schindler's name omitted. In addition, there had been some serious problems with damp at Lovell's mountain cabin, and this was perhaps enough to convince the doctor that it was time for a change of architect. Whatever the reason for his choice of Neutra, it must have made an already fraught working relationship even more difficult.

Lovell's brief was straightforward and exciting. It was to design a home that would promote a healthy lifestyle, and be the architectural embodiment of his theories and values: a "Demonstration Health House," as he called it. Neutra's response was one of the masterpieces of early twentieth-century domestic architecture, a building that did not simply match Schindler's Beach House but exceeded it in its determination to break with tradition and forge a new aesthetic for the future. Built into the hillside and looking out over Los Angeles, the Lovell House went up over the summer and autumn of 1929. It is three stories high and based on a skeletal steel frame that was erected in a record-breaking forty hours. To speed things up, standard-size metal window frames were inserted and the walls were a skin of reinforced concrete slabs that were cast on site, the concrete being taken from street level, not conventionally by wheelbarrow, but by being shot by air-compressors through hosepipes 60m (200ft) long. The exterior stucco of the building was also hosed into place.

The spaces, fluid and scarcely bounded by their enclosing materials, are oddly inverted: the entrance is at street level, but it brings one into the top floor, where there are bedrooms, dressing rooms, and sleeping porches. Descending the main staircase, one reached guest rooms and the conventional domestic apparatus – living room, dining room, kitchen, and pantry – along with an elegant and forward-looking library, with natural-colored curtains, a

BELOW For all the common-sense qualities of the design, and Lovell's earnestness about open-air living, the house benefits from a precipitous position, which gives it a poetic quality quite rare in progressive domestic architecture of the period.

grey carpet, blue upholstery, and black lacquered woodwork. Finally, one reached the healthiest part of the Demonstration Health House: the ground floor was taken up with a swimming pool, bath and shower, gymnasium, and playground. Outside were an open-air theater and courts for tennis, handball, and basketball. On the hillside below stood an avocado orchard.

If the construction methods were revolutionary, so was the appearance of the Lovell House. The steel and concrete declare themselves defiantly. Sleeping porches and balconies (both essential elements in Lovell's brief) are supported from the skeleton frame by steel cables. Projecting floors balance on slender steel stilts. The elegant International Style single-family homes that Neutra went on to design in the 1930s and 1940s – such as the William Beard House at Altadena, the Ernest Mosk House in Los Angeles, and the Kaufman Desert House in Palm Springs – established him as someone who helped to define Californian residential architecture. But the Lovell House remains a landmark in American architecture, ranking alongside the buildings of Europeans such as Le Corbusier, Behrens, and Gropius, while at the same time glorying in its rambling, picturesque, and ultimately romantic qualities. As Neutra's son Dion recalled many years later, the overall effect of the house is surreal, unearthly; it is as if "a spaceship from another planet had landed on the hillside."

ABOVE The staircase leads down from the entrance, which is on the top floor along with the bedrooms and sleeping porches, to the bright, sunlit living room, one wall of which is almost entirely glazed.

E.1027

EILEEN GRAY AND JEAN BADOVICI, 1926–9

The furniture and textiles of Eileen Gray (1878–1976) figure more than once in these pages. Gray was a designer and *ensemblier* of genius, moving with ease between High Deco and Modernism, and blurring the distinction between the two. Born into a well-to-do family in Enniscorthy, County Wexford, she left Ireland to study fine art at the Slade School in London and then moved to Paris in 1907 to be an artist. She also moved from fine art to furniture design, specializing in austere and simple lacquerwork and learning her craft with the Japanese master Sugawara. Her interest in exotic and expensive materials stood her in good stead with rich clients, and in the early 1920s she produced some stunning interiors in blacks, tans,

BELOW In a spectacular setting overlooking the Mediterranean, E.1027 is, not surprisingly, also known as "the Seaside House."

LEFT Gray and Badovici collaborated closely on their holiday home. The architecture and structural detail seem to have been Badovici's work, while it is certain that Gray both supervised the project and designed the interiors.

silvers, and greys, liberally draped with furs and animal skins. By 1922 her business was successful enough for her to open her own gallery, Jean Désert.

In 1926 Gray and her lover Jean Badovici, the critic, publisher, and editor of the forward-looking journal *L'Architecture Vivante*, decided they needed a holiday home by the sea. They chose a rocky site overlooking the Mediterranean at Roquebrune-Cap Martin, just outside the fashionable resort of Menton; and together they built E.1027. Badovici seems to have masterminded the structural niceties, but the house is essentially Gray's creation. She lived on site, supervised the building work, decorated the interiors, and designed the furnishings and textiles. It also marked a new phase in her artistic development. By the time the house was finished in 1929, she had closed Jean Désert and all but abandoned her trademark lacquerwork in favor of Modernism, tubular steel, and chrome.

E.1027 and its interiors illustrate this move away from the opulence of High Deco towards mass production, new materials, and Moderne. White, angular, and raised dramatically on stilts, the house owes a lot to Le Corbusier, whom Gray got to know well through Badovici and who became a frequent visitor: one wall of the entrance hall was given over to a magnificent mural by the architect. It also became an opportunity to experiment, a setting in which she could devise new forms and shapes; and several of her greatest pieces of furniture were created for the new house. These included adjustable chromium-plated steel tables; the famous Bibendum chair; and her even more famous Transat armchair in leather and chrome, which would later appear in New York's Museum of Modern Art.

And the peculiar name of the house? Its origin is touching, and less impersonal than it seems. It is made up of the lovers' initials intertwined and, with the exception of the E for Eileen, given numeric equivalents – J being the tenth letter of the alphabet, B the second, and G the seventh.

ABOVE The living room, with Gray's Transat chair (which was designed for the house) on the right. The large wall decoration is a marine chart.

VILLA SAVOYE

LE CORBUSIER FOR MONSIEUR AND MADAME PIERRE SAVOYE, 1928–31

Le Corbusier was born Charles-Edouard Jeanneret in the Swiss town of La Chaux-de-Fonds in 1887. The pseudonym, which he adopted in the 1920s, came from his maternal grandmother. In 1908–9 Le Corbusier worked in the Paris office of Auguste Perret, who, despite a predilection for neo-classical detailing, was then experimenting with concrete frame construction. The spell with Perret was followed by a few months in Berlin with Peter Behrens, who had just finished his pioneering AEG turbine factory in the city's Moabit district. Le Corbusier later described the glass-and-steel structure as an admirable example of "the integral architectonic creations of our time – rooms with admirable moderation and cleanness, with magnificent machines which set solemn and impressive accents."

Machines, the machine aesthetic, and the potential for standardization offered by industrial mass production continued to fascinate Le Corbusier throughout the decade between 1910 and 1920, when he worked first as an interior designer in Switzerland and then, appropriately enough, as a factory manager in Paris, while simultaneously pursuing one career as an avant-garde painter and another as an architect. In 1914 he invented a mass-produced housing unit based around a load-bearing frame, which he called "Dom-ino"; and in 1922, the year in which he set up in architectural practice with his cousin, Pierre Jeanneret, he devised a project for the Citrohan house that

ABOVE Although Le Corbusier was a leading figure of the Modern movement – with all the ideological purity that implies –many of his villas had a playful and unfunctional quality about them.

RIGHT The ground floor of Villa Savoye, where ramp, staircase, curving glass wall, and pillars combine to form a wonderfully serene composition. Who could dismiss this as merely "a machine for living in"?

could be produced on an assembly line in much the same way as a motor car. At once an astute self-publicist and an intellectual whose architecture sprang from theory rather than practice, Le Corbusier founded in 1920 the polemical review *L'Esprit Nouveau*, with the painter Amédée Ozenfant and the poet Paul Dermée. The articles he wrote for the review, collected and published as *Vers une Architecture* (1923), contained many of his most famous pronouncements on functionalism and rationality in architecture, including the frequently quoted passage in which he declared that "we have acquired a taste for clean air and full sunlight… the house is a machine for living in, bathrooms, sun, hot and cold water, temperatures which can be adjusted as required, food storage, hygiene, beauty in harmonious proportions." His five-point definition of what was required to create good modern architecture was equally famous. He declared that a building should be raised above the ground on pillars, or *pilotis*; there should be a free plan, which was achieved through the use of load-bearing columns, so that the walls were there only to subdivide space and to keep the weather out; there should be large, continuous windows, or *fenêtres en longueur*; there should be a plain façade; and the building should have a roof garden, thus restoring the area of ground lost to the house.

Given his interest in the mass production of standardized housing, it is not surprising that Le Corbusier often focused on collective housing schemes and town planning. For example, the Pavillon de l'Esprit Nouveau, which provoked strong reaction when it was shown at the 1925 Paris Exposition (see pages 46–9), was a duplex flat, a modular unit intended as part of a larger apartment block. But such projects were hard to realize, as he found in 1925–6 with his project for forty Citrohan-type workers' houses at Pessac, a

ABOVE Le Corbusier placed great importance on positioning the living rooms of the villa at second-floor level, believing that ground-floor living was unhealthy and failed to make the most of the expansive views.

ABOVE The circulation spaces provide much of the drama of Villa Savoye. The juxtaposition of railings and staircase tower inevitably remind the observer of an ocean liner.

suburb of Bordeaux: the homes were built, but the local authorities didn't approve of their advanced appearance, and refused the complex a public water supply for six years.

Individual houses were easier to bring to a successful conclusion. All one needed was a like-minded client. And so, during the 1920s, Le Corbusier and Pierre Jeanneret concentrated on creating a series of revolutionary homes. The first was Villa Ker-Ka-Re at Vaucresson, just west of Paris, a modest concrete box designed in January 1923. The last, and arguably the finest, was anything but modest. Les Heures Claires was built at Poissy, a suburb to the northwest of the capital, for the wealthy industrialist Pierre Savoye.

Le Corbusier gave Monsieur and Madame Savoye the first set of presentation drawings for their new home at the beginning of October 1928. The site was large and open, so there were none of the problems associated with small and awkward sites that had dogged several of his earlier villas. Moreover, he was given complete artistic freedom: the Savoyes were "quite without preconceived conceptions, either old or new," he later recalled. They were rich, too; but Pierre Savoye was only prepared to spend so much, and Le Corbusier's first scheme was rejected as too expensive when the estimates of 785,000 francs came in that November. The architect cut down his original scheme, and continued to experiment until just before Christmas 1928. In

February 1929 the project was estimated at 558,690 francs, and work began on the site that April. However, Le Corbusier and Jeanneret continued to alter the design in the course of construction, with unfortunate consequences for their clients' bank balance: the final cost of Villa Savoye was around 815,000 francs, forty-five percent over budget.

What did the Savoyes get for their money? A startling composition in white, an impossibly slender and elegant box that seemed to float above the ground on stilts. Le Corbusier designed the house on a five-by-five grid of *pilotis*, spaced 4.75m (15½ft) apart. In line with his five points, the walls were non-load-bearing, and the main floor was raised up, with *fenêtres en longueur* enabling the family to gaze out in all directions. On the ground floor were an entrance hall, service rooms, a three-car garage, and a guest suite. (Originally the guest suite was intended to serve as accommodation for the chauffeur, but the Savoyes changed their minds almost as soon as work on the house began, and Le Corbusier designed a separate lodge in the grounds.) The idea of living in an elevated position was very important to him, both because he thought it healthier – "the soil is unhealthy, damp" – and because it allowed the Savoyes to survey their estate and to feel part of a rural idyll. "The domestic life is inserted into a Virgilian dream," he wrote. Health, happiness, and a connection with nature were likewise the reasons for incorporating a garden terrace on the roof: "this will be the hanging garden whose surface is dry and healthy, and from it you will get a good view of the landscape, much better than if you had stayed below."

Early versions of Villa Savoye included a straight external staircase up to the second floor, symbolically linking the living area to the ground. But in the finished house, this disappeared, accentuating the "floating" quality of the building. Access to the upper floor and the garden terrace was by means of a

LEFT Internally as well as externally, the spiral staircase is one of the most striking features of the villa. Its sinuous lines subvert the machine aesthetic that Le Corbusier claimed for the new architecture.

shallow ramp that wound its way up through the center of the house, and a spiral staircase that erupted on the roof in a bravura display, disrupting the harmonies of the box.

The architect was delighted with Villa Savoye, and when the family moved in, in the spring of 1931, he advised Mme Savoye to keep a visitors' book in the entrance hall for all the illustrious people who would flock to see his latest work. The Savoyes were not so pleased, however. In the first place, Pierre was angry at the colossal overspend. But matters were made much worse by the many constructional flaws. The central heating didn't work properly, for one thing; and the building leaked badly as soon as it was finished. Despite annual running repairs and threats of legal action by the Savoyes, it continued to leak every winter, until the family got fed up and left. The house has recently been restored and is now open to the public.

Le Corbusier has been reviled as the man who stripped the life out of twentieth-century architecture, the man whose preoccupation with the machine and disregard for the human being gave birth to deserts of soulless high-rises. It may be true that his architectural ethic of the 1920s and 1930s was degraded by lesser designers, but Le Corbusier was no slave to reason and functionalism. In fact, he had a strong romantic streak. As he wrote in *Vers une Architecture*, "You employ stone, wood and concrete, and with these materials you build houses and palaces; that is construction. Ingenuity is at work. But suddenly you touch my heart, you do me good. I am happy and I say: 'This is beautiful.' That is Architecture. Art enters in." Without doubt, Art enters into Villa Savoye. Without doubt, this is beautiful.

FURNITURE DESIGN AND HIGH DECO

BELOW Eileen Gray's Transat chair in black lacquer with green leather seat and headrest and chromed-steel shoes. Gray's earliest designs for the Transat date from 1924, and it first appeared in her seaside house known as E.1027. This example, which dates from 1925–6, belonged to her lover, Jean Badovici.

The owners of an Art Deco house needed to surround themselves with more than concrete and glass in order to achieve the Deco look. While the house was merely a setting, a gallery in which to display one's wealth and modernity, the real vehicle through which they declared their allegiance to the future lay within. It was in the creation of art objects that Deco excelled.

So it is not surprising to find that many of Deco's best architects also designed furniture, or that furniture designers were inspired to dabble in architecture. Gerrit Rietveld, Pierre Chareau, and Eileen Gray are probably the most interesting examples of the latter trend; as far as the former is concerned, it would be hard to think of a significant architect in the years between the wars who didn't design furniture.

Furniture may well be the most beautiful product of High Deco. A unique, hand-crafted piece by one of the great designers, such as Jean Dunand or Jacques-Emile Ruhlmann, Eileen Gray or Clément Rousseau, was and still is an object of desire. More than this, such furniture defines perfectly the movement's eagerness to find new expressions for a luxurious, even hedonistic lifestyle in the Jazz Age. What could be more luxurious than the ebony, ivory, silk, and velvet creations of Ruhlmann? What could be more extravagant than a gleaming lacquer table by Dunand, or a chair of sharkskin and mother-of-pearl by Rousseau?

The use of exotic materials drawn from both past and present, such as shagreen and fine veneers, aluminium, and chrome, shows designers

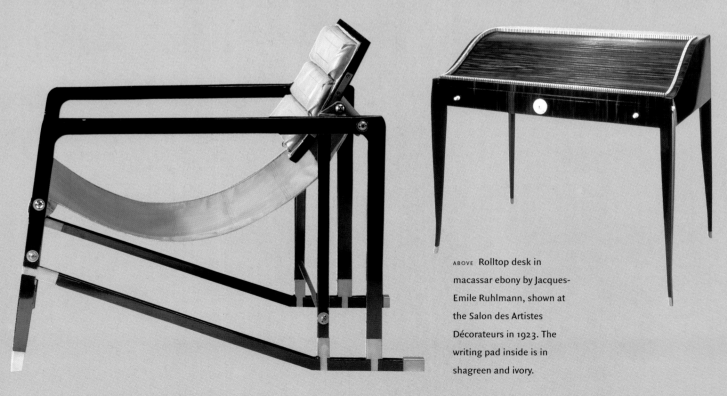

ABOVE Rolltop desk in macassar ebony by Jacques-Emile Ruhlmann, shown at the Salon des Artistes Décorateurs in 1923. The writing pad inside is in shagreen and ivory.

FAR LEFT Commode in mahogany, ebony, and shagreen with marble top, designed by Paul Iribe around 1912. The work of Iribe exemplifies early Art Deco's obsession with exotic and costly materials.

LEFT Cocktail cabinet by Maurice B. Adams, around 1934. A conservative outlook often led English furniture to lag behind its European contemporaries, but Adams, who was born in 1849, shows that old dogs could learn new tricks.

– and particularly the French designers who dominated the first wave of Deco – searching for a new, vibrant, and, above all, expensive vocabulary that impressed their nouveau-riche clientele with a richness to match their own, while at the same time seeking to re-establish France as a major player in the field of international design. To a certain extent they succeeded, although the tendency of many French cabinetmakers to cling to traditional forms, even when they were using aggressively modern decorative motifs, meant that Germany in the 1920s and the United States in the 1930s produced more innovative and challenging pieces. And the emphasis on outrageously elaborate decoration applied to simple forms offers a handy metaphor for Deco's obsession with surface, and its reluctance to engage in the social and moral dialogue so beloved by the Arts and Crafts designers of the previous generation.

Yet Art Deco furniture also exemplifies tensions that were never fully resolved but remained hidden and unacknowledged beneath the lacquer and sharkskin: tensions between the supremacy of form and the importance of function, between the drive to maintain the highest standards of craftsmanship and the moral imperative of mass production, which would make beautiful furniture available to the many. Between traditionalism and modernism, in fact.

The choices faced by the designer were clearly set out in the 1930s by the British architect Robert Gardner-Medwin. Contemporary furniture, he wrote, "is mostly of two kinds: furniture made in small quantities, taking advantage of machine technique in a limited way, but relying to a considerable extent on individual craftsmanship; and furniture made in large quantities, using machine technique from start to finish." Most classic Deco furniture produced in France fell into the first category, with a designer easing his or her social conscience (if he or she had one) by arguing for a "trickle-down" effect, which would eventually benefit everyone. "The luxury object," Ruhlmann once said, "is a stallion which helps improve the standard of mass-produced objects."

Ruhlmann was right, perhaps, but not in the way he intended: Deco furniture relied for its appeal as much on its exclusivity as its quality. Not only the standard, but also the style trickled down, and by the later 1930s, when every middle-class home could afford a cheap reproduction of a Deco sofa or table, that appeal was lost.

METROPOLIS

Urban planning, and the related issue of the multi-occupancy housing unit, have played a significant role in twentieth-century architecture. The Garden City movement pioneered by Ebenezer Howard (1850–1928) in his *Tomorrow: A Peaceful Path to Social Reform* (1898) saw fruit in Parker & Unwin's scheme for Letchworth in 1904, and Richard Riemerschmid's garden city of Hellerau. And it wasn't long before any architect worth his salt was dreaming of schemes for housing estates, planning new towns, and entire cities. Frank Lloyd Wright did it in 1915, with a Model Development for Chicago, which had evolved by 1932 into Broadacre City, and by the end of his life into the utopia of his Living City, in which each family was to be given 4000 square meters (43,000 square feet) of land. In the early 1950s Le Corbusier was involved (along with E. Maxwell Fry) in planning Chandigarh, the new capital of Punjab, India. And the New Towns planned and executed in Britain after World War II were seen as a golden opportunity to apply the principles and aspirations of the Modern movement: Berthold Lubetkin, for example, worked on Peterlee New Town in County Durham until he retired from architecture in 1950.

PREVIOUS PAGE Leslie Hotel, Miami Beach, Florida, by Albert Anis, 1937.

ABOVE The Siemensstadt estate in Berlin (1929–30) was one of the more innovative attempts at building a model settlement. The master plan was by Hans Scharoun.

BELOW In the 1930s and 1940s Streamline Moderne was in demand on the west coast of the United States for apartment buildings like this wonderful example in San Francisco.

Technology played a part in all this, and particularly the arrival of steel-frame construction and the rapid evolution of the high-rise. It was only forty-seven years from William Le Baron Jenney's ten-story Home Insurance Building in Chicago in 1883 to the seventy-seven-story Chrysler Building of William Van Alen and the 102-story Empire State (Shreve, Lamb & Harmon). The multi-occupancy apartment block, which was such an issue in architecture between the wars, was driven by technological advance. But implicit in the notion of large-scale housing design was the conviction, which was essentially Modernist, European, and left-wing, that the architect had a responsibility to work for the betterment of society. And that meant not only providing better housing and public services, but also actually creating a more efficient, planned environment; building metropolis, in other words.

So it was that some of the most interesting housing schemes of the 1920s and 1930s had their roots in this well-intentioned, if not altogether happy, desire for Big Brotherly social control. Wells Coates's Lawn Road Flats and, perhaps, Thomas Tait's Silver End Garden Village were ideologically motivated; Oud's experimental Rotterdam housing estates and Lubetkin's two Highpoint apartment blocks in Highgate, north London, even more so. But these were no drab, Stalinist blocks. The futuristic bowed ends of Oud's terraces show his understanding that it isn't only functional efficiency that makes a good building; while the caryatids supporting the entrance canopy on Lubetkin's Highpoint II introduce a note of flamboyance that his more serious-minded contemporaries found difficult to appreciate.

Most Art Deco designers had little truck with ideology. But they couldn't ignore the appeal of the planned townscape, the high-rise apartment block, the unified street scene. When there was the opportunity to produce a collection of buildings, they took it – as Rob Mallet-Stevens did at Auteuil, Paris, when he persuaded four like-minded clients to join him in buying up adjacent lots on the same street. And when the New Zealand town of Napier was devastated by an earthquake, its architects saw their chance to create a brave new world of their own.

ABOVE Norman Bel Geddes was convinced that the cities of the future would be dominated by the motor car. This 1937 scheme foresees a network of elevated sidewalks.

BELOW New York's skyline is brought to life by architects dressed as their buildings at the Hotel Astor's Beaux Arts Ball in 1931. William van Alen, as the Chrysler Building, is in the center.

KIEFHOEK HOUSING ESTATE

JACOBUS JOHANNES PIETER OUD, 1925–30

The Kiefhoek estate is one of a number of low-cost housing schemes designed between 1918 and 1933 by the Dutch architect and planner Jacobus Johannes Pieter Oud (1890–1963). None of them is ambitious in comparison with the planned towns of the post-war period; but, by providing Modernist architecture with a human persona, they have become something of an icon.

Oud trained in Amsterdam and Delft and worked as a young man with Theodor Fischer and Willem Dudok. In 1915 or 1916 he met Theo van Doesburg, and the two collaborated on several projects, notably Der Vonk, a holiday retreat for women workers at Noordwijkerhout on the North Sea. The client wanted a rigidly symmetrical and conventional building, and Oud provided a three-story house with hipped roof and gabled projecting wings that flanked the central entrance. However, this entrance was enlivened by an abstract mosaic in primary colors designed by van Doesburg. The lobby and hallway had another van Doesburg mosaic, in white, black, and yellow, while Oud took a more experimental approach to the space, creating a white staircase bounded by rectangular openings, alcoves, and stepped blocks.

Der Vonk was finished in 1918. In that year Oud, who, through van Doesburg, was now closely linked to the De Stijl artists and architects, became Rotterdam's municipal architect. The appointment, which he owed to the influence of H.P. Berlage, allowed the twenty-eight-year-old architect to put into practice his ideas on mass housing, industrialization, and standardization in architecture, and the relation between housing and urban design.

Oud's first scheme in Rotterdam was a housing estate for the western suburb of Spangen, which was built between 1918 and 1920. He must have found it a frustrating task, since his approach to architecture was radical, iconoclastic, and uncompromising: applied ornament and historicist references were to be avoided at all costs; a reverence for tradition belonged in the past; the architect's role was to find a universal formal vocabulary. But to begin with, at least, the city authorities were not prepared to give him his way and let him design truly modern buildings; and the housing blocks on the Spangen estate, which was executed in collaboration with several other architects, were, like Der Vonk, surprisingly conventional. Only apartment blocks VIII and IX, which were designed in 1919–20 and had flat roofs, plane surfaces, and recessed balconies, showed signs of Oud's theoretical position.

ABOVE The brief for the low-cost Kiefhoek estate placed great constraints on Oud, but by 1925, when he began his designs, he had enough confidence to work within those constraints instead of kicking against them.

In 1921 van Doesburg produced a colorful scheme to decorate block VIII in blues, yellows, and greens, but Oud thought this trivialized the lofty ideals of the mass-housing movement. He was already uneasy at the way in which some of his fellow artists in De Stijl, especially Gerrit Rietveld, were turning to building design without what he saw as a proper grounding in the subject. And he disagreed – quite understandably – with van Doesburg's insistence that architecture must always be subordinate to fine art. The two men fell out over Spangen, and Oud parted company with the De Stijl group.

Spangen was swiftly followed in 1920–1 by a similar housing scheme in Tusschendijken, just to the south; and then in 1922–3 by Oud-Mathenesse, a group of 343 housing units and eight shops on a narrow, triangular plot. Originally conceived as a temporary estate with a life expectancy of about twenty-five years, the white-painted wooden houses were arranged in terraces around a main square containing the shops. Despite his split with van Doesburg, Oud clearly didn't object in principle to colorful exteriors: the houses had single-pitch roofs with bright red tiles and brightly painted doors and window frames; and the project manager's house was a cubistic group of three small blocks, one painted blue, one red, and one yellow.

In 1924 Oud designed some worker housing for a large estate on the Hook of Holland. In the end only two blocks were built – they were completed in 1927 – but they are among the most famous and endearing of all Modernist domestic buildings. The development is basically two rows of terraced housing units, each two stories high, with a single balcony running the length of each block, to emphasize its horizontality; and rounded pavilions at each end.

After the Hook of Holland, Oud designed Kiefhoek, a low-cost estate to the south of Rotterdam that was intended for large families. He made his first designs in 1925, and the estate of terraced houses was built between 1928 and 1930. It shows many of the elements found in the Hook of Holland: rounded ends to the housing blocks, continuous horizontal strips, brightly painted doors and window frames.

By now Oud had the confidence and the reputation to explore his own responses to the problems of constructing low-cost housing in an industrial society, of operating within tight budgets: the Kiefhoek houses were only 4m (13ft) wide by 5m (16½ ft) deep, with three bedrooms upstairs and a living room, kitchen, and lavatory downstairs. Like that of Gropius and Le Corbusier, Oud's approach was essentially a functionalist one; and there are the elements that would soon become *de rigueur* in any functionalist building, such as flat roofs, white walls, and standardized metal window frames. But, like Gropius and Le Corbusier, Oud showed how very human functionalist architecture could be in the hands of a genius. The soulless tower blocks that were to give Modernism such a bad name had no place in his philosophy. Each unit had its own garden, although in order to maintain the identity of each block as a unit rather than as a collection of individual residences, he separated the gardens with low walls to establish uniformity. The scale of the estate is small enough for the occupants to feel that they are on a street, rather than dwellers in some futuristic metropolis. The design vocabulary still focuses on people rather than ideas.

BELOW In early black-and-white photos, which fail to show the brightly painted doors and windows, Kiefhoek can seem a little stark. But its human scale manages to redeem it in a way denied to the tower blocks of the post-war era.

RUE MALLET-STEVENS HOUSING

ROBERT MALLET-STEVENS FOR VARIOUS CLIENTS, 1926–7

"Thousands of shapes are possible," wrote Robert Mallet-Stevens (1886–1945) in a 1924 article on the possibilities offered by modern building materials. "Reinforced concrete allows cantilevering, the elimination of numerous points of support, and the reduction to a minimum of different construction elements... Now it is the whole façade rather than simply the moldings which attract the light. The architect sculpts an enormous block, the house." With the Rue Mallet-Stevens, the architect managed to sculpt an entire street, and in the process created one of the world's greatest Art Deco housing developments.

Art and architecture were in Mallet-Stevens's blood. His father, Maurice, was a valuer of paintings and one of the first to appreciate the Impressionists. In 1905 his uncle, Adolf Stoclet, commissioned a new house in Brussels from

ABOVE Robert Mallet-Stevens, seen here studying one of his own designs around 1924. Although his sense of theater kept him from full-blown functionalism, he was, after Le Corbusier, one of the most talented architects in France.

RIGHT The inauguration of the Rue Mallet-Stevens in 1927. The architect, seen in the center of the group of three, shows his creation to an assembly of suitably impressed dignitaries, including two local prefects and a government minister.

ABOVE Mallet-Stevens's
residence and office. The
three tall windows light a
duplex living hall. To the left
of this is an enclosed patio
and, on the corner of the
building, an open terrace.

Josef Hoffmann, the founder of the Wiener Werkstätte: the famous Palais
Stoclet had a profound and continuing influence on the young man's tastes.
After studying at the Ecole Spéciale d'Architecture in Paris from 1905 to
around 1910, he carved out a career for himself as a decorator and architect,
at first designing rather conventional furniture at the same time as drawing up
more modern architectural schemes. It was not until 1923 that he had an
opportunity to realize one of these projects, a villa in Hyères for the Vicomte
de Nouailles, which had interiors by several of Mallet-Stevens's friends,
including Francis Jourdain, Pierre Chareau, and Gabriel Guévrékian.

The Hyères villa helped to establish Mallet-Stevens as one of Paris's
leading avant-garde designers and led indirectly to his work at the 1925
Exposition (see pages 46–9). His Pavillon du Tourisme and the entrance hall
and winter garden he created for the Ambassade Française project attracted
much attention, and it was in the aftermath of the Exposition that the Rue
Mallet-Stevens, a cul-de-sac of six houses in Auteuil, in Paris's sixteenth
arrondissement, was conceived. With four clients interested in commissioning
town houses, the architect pulled off quite a coup by persuading them all to

buy plots in the same street, enabling him to design them as an ensemble rather than as separate entities; and throughout 1926 and 1927 he worked almost full time on this one project.

Closing off the end of the street was the caretaker's lodge: a simple, stark, white cube that reminds us why Mallet-Stevens's mature work is so often described as cubistic. The other five houses were much grander, although they varied dramatically in size. There were two substantial detached mansions on opposite sides of the street, one belonging to Madame Reifenberg and filling three plots, and the other, that of Madame Allatini, taking up two. The Maison Dreyfus, much smaller but also detached, stood next door to the Hôtel Allatini; while next to the Hôtel Reifenberg were the final two houses, which shared an adjoining wall. One was the Maison Martel, occupied by the twins Joël and Jan Martel, monumental sculptors who had created a little forest of cubist "trees" for Mallet-Stevens's garden at the 1925 Exposition. The other, which stood on the corner of the cul-de-sac and effectively advertised its designer, was the architect's own house, office, and atelier.

Mallet-Stevens introduced a number of elements that ensured that the five houses formed a coherent and identifiable group. All five fronted the street; all boasted the white walls and flat roofs, the asymmetric façades, and the windows carried unbroken around corners that announced to the world that their owners were proud members of the architectural avant-garde. Each house was composed of a series of rectilinear blocks of different sizes, piled on top of one another and set back in a series of receding planes to form terraces, sun decks, and roof gardens, with just the occasional curve to relieve the angularity. They also had more specific unifying features, such as the streamlined horizontal banding that wrapped around the base of each house, like a plinth. (Incidentally, all five houses had an integral parking garage: like Le Corbusier, Mallet-Stevens was an enthusiast of the motor car.)

But while overall stylistic similarities tied each building to its neighbors, every one was a unique composition. Mallet-Stevens's house had a sweeping open terrace at second-floor level, opening off a roofed patio, which in turn led through to a large living room. (As with the adjacent Maison Martel, the ground floor was largely occupied by workshop and offices.) The Martel brothers' house was distinguished by a spiral, cantilevered staircase that snaked around an open stairwell, starting on the ground floor and rising the full height of the building until it emerged on the roof – and then continued for another 3m (10ft) until it came to rest in a little sun deck beneath a circular, toadstool-like canopy. The roofline of the Hôtel Reifenberg was characterized by an arrangement of chimneystacks formed from paper-thin concrete sheets; the Hôtel Allatini was austere, block-like; and the Maison Dreyfus was topped with a curious rectilinear concrete roof canopy.

Mallet-Stevens employed an impressive list of craftsmen on the project. There were the Martel twins, one of whose sculpted mirrors hung in the architect's hall. The entrances were designed by Prouvé, and the interiors by a stable of artists – Mallet-Stevens himself, Noémi Hesse, Pierre Chareau, and Francis Jourdain (both of whom had designed furniture for the Pavillon du Tourisme), and Gabriel Guévrékian, a Turkish-born decorator and architect who also supervised the building work. Mallet-Stevens's tastes veered

BELOW The interior of the Martel twins' house, which was next door to Mallet-Stevens's. The entrance hall, dominated by one of the Martels' abstract sculptures, displays a glorious combination of curves and angles.

between Deco and a pure, almost minimalist form of Modernism, and the furnishings of his own house reflected this. There was a desk by Chareau, tubular-steel Bauhaus chairs from Marcel Breuer's workshop at Dessau, Germany, carpets from Fernand Léger, and textiles by Hélène Henry.

One of the most distinctive decorative features of the street were the tall, slender windows filled with stained glass in strongly geometrical, abstract patterns, all the work of the artist Louis Barillet. In the Reifenberg house one of his bright slits of color rose as a continuous strip through four stories, illuminating the staircase; the circular stairwell in the Martels' villa was likewise lit all the way up by a Barillet window; and the façade of Mallet-Stevens's house was dominated by three tall strips of Barillet glass, which lit the double-height hall and provided an important vertical counterpoint to the horizontal lines that otherwise might overpower the exterior. Barillet was one of Mallet-Stevens's favorite collaborators. His stained glass had adorned the Pavillon du Tourisme, and in 1932, five years after the Rue Mallet-Stevens was opened with great ceremony by a government minister, the architect would design a combined town house and workshop for the artist at 15 Square Vergennes in the fifteenth arrondissement.

ABOVE This early photograph of the Martels' villa shows Louis Barillet's stained glass in the window that lights the circular staircase turret. Notice the horizontal streamlining around the lower walls, a feature common to every house in the Rue Mallet-Stevens.

SILVER END GARDEN VILLAGE

THOMAS S. TAIT, 1927–8

I n 1928 the *Architectural Review* published a lengthy survey of recent English domestic architecture, featuring photographs and plans of eighty-one contemporary houses. They were arranged according to style, beginning with timber-framed mock-Tudor and Jacobethan, and moving on to Wrenaissance and neo-Georgian. Finally, at the end of the survey, there was a tiny group of five houses that resolutely refused to be placed in the past. One was Peter Behrens's New Ways in Northampton (see pages 60–3). Like New Ways, the other four were quite unlike traditional English homes. They all had flat roofs, sharp angles, and strong horizontals, and made no attempt to evoke the vernacular: the ivory-colored walls were plain and sheer, as though intended to keep their occupants cool and protected from the burning heat of the sun; and there were balconies protected with bright awnings. They were all designed by Thomas S. Tait, and all at Silver End, about 16km (10 miles) northeast of Chelmsford, Essex.

One of the earliest and most intriguing manifestations of modern European architecture to appear in Britain, Silver End Garden Village was the brainchild of Francis Crittall (later Lord Braintree), whose company made

ABOVE Francis Crittall, an Essex ironmonger who grew rich after becoming a manufacturer of metal window frames, was an enlightened employer who set out to provide a model village for his workers.

RIGHT Thomas S. Tait, the architect of Silver End, was heavily influenced by Peter Behrens's New Ways of 1924–5. The triangular glass bay projecting over a flat canopy is a direct borrowing from the earlier house.

metal windows. Crittall conceived Silver End in 1926 as both a showpiece for the firm's products and a planned settlement for workers – many of them disabled war veterans – at a new Crittall factory. The housing was mixed, as befitted this purpose-built community, and there was a church and a welfare club for staff. A terrace of four three-bedroomed "cottages," each with sitting room, living room, and scullery, was erected for a total cost of £2412 ($1507). More ambitious were four-bedroom detached houses ranging from £1250 to £2000 ($780–$1250) and presumably intended for senior members of the Crittall staff; these had connected garages and good-sized rooms, and showed more attention to detailing. Grandest of all was the £3000 ($1870) house, which – perhaps in homage to its continental origins – was called Le Château. Looking forward to the Liner Style of the 1930s, it was sleek and elegant, the horizontal lines of its roofs and balconies emphasized by Crittall steel casement windows without vertical glazing bars.

Silver End's Modernism was, however, only skin deep. While most of the buildings had flat roofs and plain walls, the walls were, in fact, built traditionally of brick and either rendered or simply color-washed. There were some overtly Deco details, such as slender, triangular oriel windows (borrowed directly from New Ways), stylized zigzag patterns to balconies and other ironwork, and geometric motifs in the glass of the front doors. Most of the metalwork, including the Crittall windows, was painted emerald green.

Tait went on to design several other interesting buildings, including the white ziggurat of The Haven in Newbury, Berkshire (1929), which also showed his considerable debt to Behrens and New Ways; and the spectacular 76m (250ft) high Empire Tower, the centerpiece of the 1938 Glasgow Exhibition, which achieved the feat of mixing Art Deco with Russian Constructivism.

ABOVE "I saw a pleasant village of a new order," wrote the industrialist Francis Crittall; "a contented community of Crittall families enjoying the amenities of town life in a lovely rural setting."

MIAMI BEACH

HENRY HOHAUSER AND OTHERS, 1930–40

The man usually credited with putting Miami Beach, Florida, on the map is Carl Fisher (1874–1939), a charismatic character with an entrepreneurial flair and a fortune made from selling his Prest-O-Lite car-headlight business to Union Carbide in 1909. Between 1913 and 1920 Fisher dredged Biscayne Bay and created an island of 19 square kilometers (7.4 square miles) with a beach 13km (8 miles) long. A causeway connecting Miami Beach with the mainland was completed in 1920; and over the next five years the population grew by 440 percent. As real-estate prices rocketed, Fisher's personal wealth grew to nearly $100 million by 1925.

Miami Beach, and particularly South Beach, quickly acquired a reputation as a holiday resort for wealthy Midwesterners. That reputation was dented, first by a hurricane that hit the city in September 1926, then by adverse press coverage that hinted darkly at shady land deals, and finally by the Wall Street Crash of 1929, which caused the stream of well-to-do tourists to dry up and cost Fisher his fortune. But Miami Beach bounced back; and

BELOW Designed in 1936, this apartment building on Pennsylvania Avenue is one of Henry Hohauser's most delightful small-scale designs, although the projection over the central window is rather odd.

on South Beach between 1934 and 1940 scores, if not hundreds, of new hotels sprang up, along with cinemas, restaurants and bars, public buildings, department stores, and apartment blocks. And many of them were in Miami Beach's own brand of Moderne. Flat roofs, fins, and decorative bands of parallel lines abound. There are flat concrete canopies and zigzags and blocky Mayan motifs; glass blocks and vitrolite; stepped-back silhouettes and nautical rails and streamlined curving bays. Indeed Miami Beach possesses the finest and most cohesive collection of Art Deco architecture in the world.

When the area began to grow in the 1920s, its preferred style was actually an ornate Spanish or Mediterranean Revival, which, with its suggestion of sunny and exotic lands, was felt to be appropriate for the new resort. That its tastes moved so wholeheartedly towards Art Deco was partly a matter of timing – the building boom in Miami Beach took place just as Moderne was reaching its gloriously vulgar peak in America – and partly one of personalities. Local people tended to stick with the Mediterranean style that was familiar and comfortable to them, although by the decade's end stripped classical was starting to compete, and even Spanish Revival buildings were sporting the occasional ziggurat outline. But the entrepreneurs and money men who saw the investment potential of the Beach were progressive East Coasters, with more advanced tastes than the native Floridians. The architects they commissioned were like-minded men and, while by the early 1930s there were scores of designers working on South Beach projects, the dominant figures were all enthusiasts for the new style.

ABOVE **The Breakwater Hotel, with its distinctive angular concrete tower, is a masterpiece of Streamline Moderne. The building, on Ocean Drive, was designed in 1939 by Anton Skislewicz.**

Henry Hohauser is the architect who introduced Miami Beach to full-blown Moderne. Aged thirty-seven when he arrived there in 1932, he had worked for some years in the New York practice of his cousin William Hohauser, and it was while he was in William's office, watching the skyline being transformed by classic Art Deco skyscrapers like the Chrysler and the Empire State, that he developed a passion for Modernism and the Moderne.

One of Hohauser's early commissions, the Crescent Hotel (1932) on Ocean Drive (see jacket image), was already intent on showing Miami Beach how its architecture could entertain the tourists. A playful piece of Moderne, it has features typical of the style and the period: the flat roofs and projecting flat canopies to the windows, with horizontal banding introduced at frequent but irregular intervals. But then a parallel pair of streamline bands shoot up one side of the building to curve around an upper corner of the façade – before stopping abruptly. Other external decoration is just as arbitrary. The bands are followed up the building by a curious line of raised ornament that continues right along the roofline; and a horizontal row of six small raised roundels gives way to a much larger circle containing a plaster sunburst.

Hohauser was prolific, eventually designing more than 300 buildings in the Miami Beach area. In 1936 alone he built seven major hotels, including the Taft, which has some wonderfully idiosyncratic Mayan-inspired decoration. And there is no doubt that his facility to produce witty and enigmatic architecture at a staggering rate contributed to the creation of a Deco culture on the Beach. But other gifted architects were just as productive.

BELOW Miami Beach's most flamboyant Deco structures were the hotels that catered to tourists. Yet even modest apartment buildings, such as this 1936 example by M.J. Nadel, show what a potent force the style became.

L. Murray Dixon, who arrived in Miami in 1928 and remained for eighteen years, designed forty hotels, eighty-seven apartment houses, thirty-three stores, and 229 residences. Some of them were forgettable; others, like the Tyler (1937), the Kent (1939) and the Haddon Hall (1941), were masterpieces of Moderne. Albert Anis, who was described by Barbara Baer Capitman, the late historian and champion of the Deco District, as having "the greatest flair for unrestrained flamboyancy and fantasy of any of the group," contributed gems like the streamlined Poinciana (1939) and the spectacular neon tower that gave the Waldorf Towers (1937) its name.

By 1940 Hohauser, Dixon, Anis, and their colleagues had established a distinctive Miami Deco, a seaside architecture that used stylized palms, birds, and other motifs drawn from the locality and blended them with the fastest, loudest, brashest form of Streamline Moderne.

However, by the late 1970s, Miami Beach's Art Deco heritage had been neglected for decades, and major monuments were being routinely destroyed. Hohauser's magnificent Moderne New Yorker Hotel was demolished in 1980, followed two years later by his Neron on Washington Avenue; Anis's Poinciana was pulled down in 1988. Fortunately, the heroic efforts of local preservationists have succeeded in getting an area of 2.5 square kilometers (1 square mile) of the city added to the National Register of Historic Places. The creation of the Art Deco District, while not guaranteeing the stringent statutory regulation that listed buildings in Britain can expect, has at least saved some of Miami Beach's Deco architecture.

NAPIER

C.T. NATUSCH & SONS, J.A. LOUIS HAY, FINCH & WESTERHOLM, E.A. WILLIAMS, AND OTHERS, 1931

At 10:46 on the morning of Tuesday, February 3, 1931, the little town of Napier, on New Zealand's North Island, was shaken by an earthquake that measured 7.9 on the Richter Scale. When it ended two and a half minutes later, 258 people were dead or dying; the center of Napier was in ruins; and the entire area had tilted some 2m (6ft), instantly reclaiming around 1090 hectares (2700 acres) of swampland. Within moments, broken gas pipes caught fire; broken water pipes meant that a shocked and dazed population could do little to put out the flames; and much of what had survived the earthquake went up in smoke.

It was two years before the town was able to celebrate its reconstruction with the New Napier Carnival of January 1933. And by an accident of timing and circumstance, the dramatic destruction of this little settlement in one of the remotest countries on earth led to the creation of an Art Deco city, one of the world's great monuments to Deco.

BELOW Once the Art Deco tradition had begun in the rebuilt town of Napier, it was hard to halt. This delightful two-story house dates from 1950, making it an unusually late example of the style.

In 1931 Napier, with a population of only 30,000, had no fewer than four architectural practices, and, unsurprisingly, these varied in both the quality of the work they produced and the stylistic predilections of their partners. The most senior was that of C.T. Natusch & Sons, whose founder, Charles Tilleard Natusch, had emigrated to New Zealand in 1886 after training in England. He had an established country-house practice in Napier and Wellington and produced some very English, vaguely Arts and Crafts homes in the area between 1910 and 1930. His three sons, Aleck, Rene, and Stanley, were all working for the family firm at the time of the earthquake; Stanley, who had spent some time in England in the 1920s, was the proud owner of three folios of photographs from the 1925 Paris Exposition.

One of Natusch's pupils, J.A. Louis Hay, had also set up business in Napier. He was a passionate enthusiast for the work of Frank Lloyd Wright and, as a result, the town had seen some rather incongruous Prairie School buildings erected in the 1920s. The third Napier practice was that of Walter P. Finch, who was considered rather staid; in the aftermath of the earthquake, however, he went into partnership with the more advanced H.A. Westerholm, who was a fan of the Spanish Mission style then popular in California. London-born E.A. Williams, who had opened an office in Napier in 1912, was perhaps the least restrained of the four: certainly, it was he who designed the most exciting Art Deco in the new Napier.

In the weeks after the earthquake Natusch & Sons, Hay, Finch & Westerholm, and E.A. Williams banded together to form Napier Associated

ABOVE Most houses put up in the aftermath of the Napier earthquake were modest, single-story buildings. Local regulations stipulated that garden walls should be no higher than 1m (3ft) so that residential areas would maintain an open appearance.

Architects, with Rene Natusch as chairman. In late 1933 J.T. Watson arrived
to become Borough Architect; having worked in the United States, he was,
like Williams, a fan of the latest in Art Deco. These men were largely
responsible for the reconstruction of Napier; and, while each followed his
own fancy, the general tendency was towards Deco.

New Zealand already had a small but healthy tradition of building Art
Deco architecture in 1931. Fostered by Hollywood as much as by the avant-
garde architectural press, flat-roofed, white-walled, faintly futuristic homes
were springing up in suburbs all over the country, and they can still be seen
around Auckland and other major cities. Indeed the style had already made
an appearance in Napier, in the zigzag and sunburst decoration of
Westerholm's Hurst's Building of 1930. It wasn't the only style chosen for the
reconstruction – Finch & Westerholm's Spanish Mission found a place, as did
a kind of austere free classicism that was favored by the Natusch brothers.
But Art Deco dominated, although it went under various names: in the new
suburb of Marewa, for example, which was developed from the reclaimed
swamp (Marewa means "gift from the sea" in the Maori language), there was
a proliferation of "Spanish bungalows" that had little to do with Spain and
everything to do with Deco.

The most interesting examples in Napier itself were public and
commercial, a reflection of Art Deco's global appeal to the builders of office

blocks and cinemas. E.A. Williams's Daily Telegraph Building (1932), the façade of which incorporates a gloriously unscholarly Deco version of a Corinthian order, was among the best. The same architect's Hawke's Bay Chambers (1932), with a distinctive chevron glazing pattern and a rectilinear, radiator-grille façade, and J.T. Watson's Municipal Theatre (1938), with chrome fittings, leaping nudes, and cubist carpets, follow close behind. In the 1950s, when Napier's Art Deco heritage was about as welcome as an earthquake, the director of the local museum wrote that, aesthetically, Watson's Theatre "can only be described as regrettable."

The Spanish bungalows of Marewa represent the Art Deco house at its most intimate and most endearing. Small-scale and ordinary, Marewa Deco is a world away from the exclusivist flights of fancy of Ruhlmann and Chareau, or the Modernist experiments of Mendelsohn and Chermayeff. Yet their stepped walls and sunburst ironwork, the abstract motifs in low relief that decorate their walls – lozenges and lines, zigzags and curves and triangles – proclaim their pedigree and tie them unmistakably to the same architectural tradition.

Interestingly, the presence of so much Art Deco in Napier and its suburbs owed less to the influence of any one architect than to post-earthquake practicalities. In the aftermath of the disaster, simple reinforced-concrete box construction was considered the most sensible option, because concrete buildings were quick and easy to produce and had stood up to the earthquake better than anything else. Moreover, the sort of low-relief ornament that Art Deco could offer wouldn't drop off and kill anybody; a number of fatalities had been caused by falling masonry. This is surely the only time in the bold, brash, elitist history of Art Deco architecture that the style was chosen because it was cheap, safe, and functional.

BELOW A pair of houses on Georges Drive shows why Art Deco proved so popular with Napier residents and architects alike. With a little imagination and at minimal cost, simple, cubistic boxes could be turned into fashionable residences.

LAWN ROAD FLATS

WELLS COATES FOR ISOKON, 1933

Wells Coates (1895–1958), the Canadian architect who designed the pioneering reinforced-concrete block of flats in Lawn Road, London, was a gifted designer, whose work ranged from bakelite door handles, electric fires, and wireless sets to futuristic control panels for BBC studios and the interior decoration of the London home of the actors Charles Laughton and Elsa Lanchester. In 1929 he met Jack and Molly Pritchard, whose furniture firm, Isokon, had bought a building site in Lawn Road and commissioned another architect to design a conventional neo-Georgian house. It wasn't quite what they were looking for, and Coates, whose commitment to Modernism matched their own, promised them something far more exciting.

The initial scheme involved two houses, one of which was meant for the Pritchards, and a single-story nursery school. Over the next four years this evolved until, when it was finally begun in September 1933, it had become a

ABOVE Wells Coates, who once described the central aims of architecture as "the provision of ordered shelter and an aspect of significance in the arrangement of buildings."

RIGHT Although the flats proved hard to let, they boasted some illustrious tenants, including Walter Gropius, Marcel Breuer, Agatha Christie, and Henry Moore's wife, Irina.

four-story apartment block consisting of twenty-two single flats, each with a bed-sitting room, a bathroom, and a tiny kitchenette; four double flats, in which a separate sleeping area was screened off from the living room by a sliding partition, and three studio flats. The Pritchards had a penthouse of their own, and there were staff quarters and offices on the ground floor. As well as a lack of ornament, a determination to dispense with the past, and an innovative use of concrete, one of the most interesting features of the block was the way in which external galleries gave access to the single flats.

Each flat was centrally heated and provided with basic furniture, much of it built-in. There was a table, a divan, a dressing table, fitted cupboards, linoleum on the floor, and a well-equipped modern kitchenette with an electric cooker and a refrigerator. For those tenants who found the prospect of fending for themselves rather too modern, cleaning, bedmaking, and even shoe-polishing were provided, while the service kitchen on the ground floor delivered hot meals to the door on demand.

Coates fell out with the Pritchards almost as soon as the Lawn Road Flats were completed. He felt that they had claimed too much of the credit for the development – a grievance which Jack Pritchard acknowledged to be true years later. In the meantime the revolutionary and un-English design made the flats difficult to let, although the situation became easier in 1939, when their reinforced-concrete construction made them seem more attractively bombproof than conventional housing.

In 1946 the magazine *Horizon* summed up British antipathies towards modern architecture when it awarded the block second prize in a competition to find the ugliest building in Britain.

ABOVE External galleries built out from the side of the main block provided access to the single flats, a feature that was borrowed by post-war architects with much less happy results.

HIGHPOINT I AND II

BERTHOLD LUBETKIN/TECTON, 1933–5, 1936–8

Like most of the best Modernist designers operating in Britain in the 1930s, Berthold Lubetkin (1901–90) had a cosmopolitan background. The architect responsible for Highpoint I and Highpoint II was born in Georgia. He was a student in Moscow in the heady days immediately following the October Revolution, before pursuing his architectural studies in Germany and Poland. In 1925 he settled in Paris, where he helped to set up Konstantin Melnikov's Soviet Pavilion at the Exposition and made friends with Le Corbusier. Lubetkin remained for six years in France, where his only important commission was the avant-garde apartment building at 25 Avenue de Versailles in Paris, which he designed in collaboration with Jean Ginsberg in 1928–31.

In 1931 the Soviet government asked him to look for suitable British architects who might take part in the competition to design the Palace of the Soviets in Moscow. A committed Communist, he traveled to London and ended up staying there. It was there that he formed Tecton, a cooperative practice in partnership with six idealistic young British architects: Anthony Chitty, Lindsay Drake, Michael Dugdale, Valentine Harding, Godfrey Samuel, and Francis Skinner. Tecton made its debut in 1933 with London Zoo's Gorilla House, a commission followed over the next six years by thirteen zoological buildings, including the famous Penguin Pool at London Zoo (1934), the British public's first serious introduction to Modernist architecture.

It was also in 1933 that Lubetkin was introduced to Sigmund Gestetner, son of the founder of the successful office-equipment company of that name. Initially interested in providing housing for his workers, Gestetner had become intrigued with the idea of collective apartment-block accommodation, a revolutionary concept in Britain in the early 1930s. The industrialist agreed with his architect that they would put up a simple, low-cost block of flats and a suitable site was found in Highgate – the healthiest place in London and "less than thirty minutes from the City and the West End," according to Gestetner's promotional literature. He stipulated that he needed an annual return of eight percent on his investment.

The result was Highpoint I, one of the concrete icons of the Modern movement in Britain. It consisted of forty-eight flats on six floors, laid out in a double cruciform plan with four two-bedroom and four three-bedroom flats on each floor. The ground floor was intended as communal space, with garages in the basement, spectacular views over the surrounding countryside, and sliding windows to make the most of them: if the workers had been left behind at some point in the development of the stripped-down, supremely

ABOVE Lubetkin later recalled that "Highpoint I was designed at a time when the most fundamental changes in society seemed necessary ... it seemed that nothing worse could happen and that we could change everything for the better."

functional design, it was still a brilliant attempt to reconcile the bourgeoisie to collective housing and was described at the time as "one of the finest, if not absolutely the finest, middle-class housing projects in the world."

In 1936 Lubetkin persuaded Gestetner to buy the adjacent house and replace it with a second apartment block, Highpoint II. Since the first Highpoint had been designed, Tecton had undergone some radical changes, the most notable being that Chitty, Dugdale, Harding, and Skinner had left, exasperated at Lubetkin's autocratic management style. More significantly, resistance to the new architecture had hardened over the past couple of years. Residents had formed a Highgate Preservation Society to ensure that experiments like Highpoint I were not repeated (in their backyard, at least); and the local Council was now adamant that any new block on the site must "preserve the architectural character of the neighborhood."

Lubetkin used some ingenious subterfuges to get his plans passed by the Council. Convinced that they would not be approved if it was known that they came from Tecton, he had them submitted by a front man, and contrived to imply in the presentation drawings that he was still trying to decide between various highly orthodox alternatives. In the end permission was obtained for the new block, although with an important proviso: it was to be only six stories high, plus penthouse, and there were to be just twelve two-story, four-bedroom maisonettes. This meant that in order for Gestetner to obtain a decent return on his investment, the apartments in Highpoint II must command much higher rents than those in Highpoint I. And they did. There

RIGHT The garden façade of Highpoint II. Lubetkin deliberately created a stark contrast between the more solid "wings" of the apartment block (one of which is shown here) and the light, open spaces of the central section.

were separate tradesmen's entrances and lifts, and backstairs for the servants, whose rooms were on the ground floor. In a revealing set of drawings prepared by one of the Tecton draughtsmen, a pinafored maid is seen opening the door to a visitor, and deliverymen arrive with groceries while a servant prepares food and the family sits at the dining table drinking coffee.

The purists were uneasy. Designing luxury apartments for rich people might be all right for the architects of High Deco, but the new generation of Modernists were supposed to be defined by their social commitment, their mission to find the Holy Grail of cheap, functional housing for workers. But if the apartheid of separate circulation systems for tenants and servants was disturbing, the unease spilled over into outright condemnation when it came to Lubetkin's treatment of the entrance to Highpoint II. A canopy projects out from the main block in a sweeping curve: one end is cantilevered, but in an extraordinary departure from his minimalist aesthetic, the architect hit on the notion of supporting the other end of the canopy on two classical caryatids that were cast from molds obtained from the British Museum. The effect is memorable but unfortunate, and the decision attracted much criticism.

Unabashed, Lubetkin moved into the penthouse flat in Highpoint II as soon as it was completed in 1938, and with his wife Margaret he designed the furniture and interior decoration. The overall impression was of controlled opulence, of straight lines and right angles marshaled to the cause of comfortable living. The same might be said of the entire Highpoint group. A sense of flight from the earth achieved in solid concrete is how it was described by the landscape designer Geoffrey Jellicoe, a long-time tenant.

ABOVE A contemporary photograph of Lubetkin's luxurious penthouse flat in Highpoint II. The sofa and chairs were made by the architect and his wife, using Norwegian yew and Argentinian cow hide.

LOS ANGELES APARTMENT BUILDINGS

MILTON J. BLACK, C.1939

Los Angeles feels like the home of Streamline Moderne. Hollywood's happy obsession with the style, both in movies and in real life, led to a huge number of important and not-so-important forays into Deco. Some of the better-known examples range from Claude Beelman's Bankers Building (1930), a study in glass and shiny green tiles, to Gordon Kaufmann's 1935 Los Angeles Times Building. More obviously Moderne-ist work includes Robert V. Derrah's Coca-Cola Building (1937); Coulter's department store (Stiles O. Clements, 1937); and, best of all, S. Charles Lee's Academy Theater (1939). This last was topped with a 38m (125ft) high, blue-neon helter-skelter of a spiral, and looked more like a set for the Flash Gordon series than the setting for Saturday-morning screenings of the show.

Milton J. Black was a prolific, although largely unsung, hero of the Los Angeles building scene in the 1930s, an architect who could turn his hand to different styles and different building types. His 1938 hot-dog stand on San Vicente Boulevard is acknowledged today as something of a classic in a genre that, until the advent of fast food, was largely overlooked; and his Spanish

ABOVE AND RIGHT Looking like something out of Raymond Chandler, this building was one of Milton J. Black's more ambitious essays in Moderne. And it works, demonstrating that the style could offer visually exciting alternatives to the high-rise apartment block.

Colonial Revival multi-level apartment building on South Burnside Avenue, with its cascade of tiled roofs, was designated a Historic-Cultural Monument by Los Angeles City Council in 1989.

However, Black's heart lay with the Moderne, of which he was a master. Both of the buildings shown here date from the late 1930s or early 1940s, when the style was at its peak in Los Angeles. And both are apartment buildings rather than individual residences. This is interesting in itself: we tend to think of the term "apartment building" as synonymous with "high-rise" – especially in the America of the 1930s – and forget that the long, sweeping Liner Style was just as potent an image as the skyscraper.

These two apartment blocks show different approaches. The building illustrated above is quite modest, in spite of the sun decks, the recessed verandahs, and the vertical radiator-grille, which dominates the wing closest to the street and declares its provenance as stridently as a manifesto. It could almost be a substantial suburban house of the 1930s in Brighton or Birmingham in England, or in Berlin.

The building shown on the opposite page is a much more ambitious project. The windows maintain a sense of continuity and establish the three separate levels on which the building operates, in spite of the variations in shape and size. But the visual anchor that they provide is vital, because the rest of the composition dissolves into a series of blocks and balconies, ribbed curves, semi-circular terraces, and flat, concrete canopies. Black contrives to make the different elements of the building look like the architectural counterpart of the mid-twentieth-century community – at once disparate, different, separate, unique, and, ultimately, at odds with one another. But still joined at the hip, still part of a larger whole. That is quite an achievement.

ABOVE As with the example opposite, this apartment building incorporates a vertical radiator-grille motif. Here Black extends it above the roofline, like a giant seam that holds the main block together.

FAIR PLAY

Art Deco is well suited to the architecture of exhibitions and expositions. One has only to think of great sights of the 1920s and 1930s such as Robert Mallet-Stevens's Pavillon du Tourisme at the 1925 Paris Exposition (see pages 46–9) or Thomas S. Tait's metal tower at Glasgow's 1938 Empire Exhibition. To draw crowds, an exhibition pavilion must be dramatic, spectacular, unusual – all qualities that Deco and Moderne possessed in plenty. Moreover, ever since London's Great Exhibition of 1851, international expositions have celebrated contemporary culture. Past achievements may be remembered, but future sales are what really count. This futuristic viewpoint also made Moderne a good choice for pavilion architecture, and the dozens of big fairs and exhibitions held in Europe and America between the wars relied heavily on Deco design.

The great Texas Centennial Exposition may not be the most famous of these events, but it left one of the most interesting legacies. It was intended to mark the hundredth anniversary of the state's independence from Mexico, and opened in Fair Park, Dallas, on 6 June 1936. After years of negotiation and some keen competition, Dallas was chosen as the venue over more historic rivals for the simple reason that the city agreed to put up more money than anyone else. Many of the exposition buildings have survived, from the Dallas Aquarium to the Museum of Natural History and the Horticulture Center, while Fair Park, now a National Historic Landmark, claims to have "the largest collection of 1930s Art Deco exposition style architecture in the United States."

There were fifty buildings in all, put up by an army of 8000 workers. Although there was an

BELOW Yellow rays of Texas: the nightly spectacular display in the main esplanade of the Centennial Exhibition bore a remarkable resemblance to an Art Deco sunburst.

overall Moderne feel to the entire site, the styles in fact varied considerably. The main administration building was stripped classical; as the official guide explained, "it has the air of modern simplicity and classic severity which is typical of the Twentieth Century." Equally restrained was the monumental-classical Varied Industries, Electrical, and Communications Building, which was designed by the Exposition's coordinating architect, George L. Dahl. This was a severe block-like structure that wouldn't have looked out of place in Mussolini's Rome: it was home to, among other things, a Dallas department store, a Czechoslovakian souvenir stall, and a Coca-Cola bottling plant, which drew the crowds while at the same time catering to the many vending machines dotted around the site.

More exuberant was the Livestock Building, which was also designed by George L. Dahl. But pride of place went to the $1.25 million Hall of State, designed by Donald Bartheleme. Huge murals in the Great Hall, painted by New York artist Eugene Savage, show memorable scenes from Texan history; and the Hall of Heroes has bronze statues by Pompeo Coppini, depicting six figures who were instrumental in the formation of the Republic of Texas, including Sam Houston, the first president of the Republic, and William B. Travis, who commanded at the Alamo in 1836.

One of the most popular attractions was a "Cavalcade of Texas," a historical pageant showing 400 years of the Lone Star State's history. The twin themes were history and progress; and the juxtaposition was perfectly illustrated on the

LEFT AND BELOW Even before the Exposition opened, Dahl's magnificient Federal Building, which stood at the end of the main esplanade, was hailed as one of its most beautiful pieces of architecture. Built at a cost of around $325,000, the building's sleek tower beckoned visitors into a star-spangled interior where they saw "The Story of Life," described in 1936 as "one of the greatest scientific exhibits of the century."

cover of the souvenir guidebook, which showed a smiling cowgirl in leather chaps astride a rearing horse, while in the background searchlights flashed across the night sky and the brightly colored geometrical shapes of uniformly futuristic exposition buildings beckoned.

The Centennial Exposition closed on 29 November 1936. Although it attracted 6,345,385 visitors, this number fell short of expectations, not least because nearly a million others were drawn to Fort Worth, which, after it failed to win the main event, insisted on holding its own unofficial Centennial Exposition with the theme of "the Winning of the West." The Fair Park buildings were put to use again the following year, however, when Dallas hosted the Greater Texas and Pan American Exposition. Today the site regularly hosts the State Fair, and buildings are still being added; the most recent is the cruciform-shaped African American Museum, which opened in 1993.

UN-ENGLISH
AND UNMANLY

Make a list of the most exciting architects working in Britain between the wars, and who have you got? Peter Behrens, probably, and Berthold Lubetkin. Ernö Goldfinger would be there. So would Walter Gropius, who spent three years in London after he fled the Nazis in 1934. And we couldn't leave out Erich Mendelsohn or Serge Chermayeff. A German, a Russian, a Hungarian, two more Germans, and another Russian (although admittedly, Chermayeff was a naturalized British citizen). Let's try again. What about Wells Coates? Canadian. Amyas Connell? A New Zealander, like his partner Basil Ward. William Lescaze? A Geneva-born American.

The new architecture was unpopular with the native architectural establishment, which regarded it as un-English, unmanly, too "artistic." But it had its champions, such as E. Maxwell Fry, the dedicated follower of Modernism who took Gropius into partnership in 1934; and Joseph Emberton, whose concrete-and-glass Royal Corinthian Yacht Club at Burnham-on-Crouch, Essex (1930–1), was a rare instance of nautical Liner Style Moderne applied in an appropriate context. And few architects could be more British and more modern than the dashing major Oliver Hill, who emerged from the war with a Military Cross and from the 1925 Paris Exposition with a passion for the avant-garde.

But they were exceptions. Modern architecture was viewed with suspicion in Britain. Its contempt for the past disturbed an older generation that was either still locked into the dreamy anti-industrial utopias of Morris and the Arts and Crafts movement, or was happy to carry on along a neo-classical, neo-Georgian path laid down for it before World War I by Edwin Lutyens, Richard Norman Shaw, and Reginald Blomfield. Herbert Baker, Lutyens's partner on the monumental-classical New Delhi project, spoke for many when he complained, as J.M. Barrie had done before him, that the battle cry of the younger generation was "Whatever was, is wrong."

PREVIOUS PAGE **High Cross House**, Dartington, Devon, by George Howe & William Lescaze, 1931–2.

BELOW In 1934 Frinton-on-Sea, Essex, was to be the site of an 1100-house development. The scheme foundered and this house by Oliver Hill was one of only a handful to be built.

BELOW Britain scorned avant-garde European architecture. Yet, for the seaside, the latest in Streamline Moderne, such as Joseph Emberton's 1930s station at Blackpool, seemed the perfect choice.

LEFT The De La Warr Pavilion, at Bexhill, Sussex, remains one of Britain's few Modernist icons. It was designed in 1934 by Eric Mendelsohn and Serge Chermayeff, who stirred British Fascists to denounce "the contemptible and despicable betrayal of our own countrymen."

BELOW *Punch* magazine pokes fun at modern architecture in this 1936 cartoon. The house is a polyglot composition, but the mushroom-shaped water tower was a prominent and unpopular feature of Amyas Connell's striking Modernist creation High and Over.

Then there was the politics of modern architecture: left-wing, idealistic, and pro-Soviet. Modernist architects were impatient to change the world; they saw themselves as vital to the task of reshaping society in a more equitable fashion; and, like the Nazis, their conservative colleagues associated Communism with Modernism and hated both in equal measure. And many of them were as xenophobic and anti-Semitic as the Nazis, identifying the new architecture as foreign and Jewish – and therefore necessarily bad. When Mendelsohn and Chermayeff won the competition to design the De La Warr Pavilion at Bexhill, Sussex, in 1934, the decision caused an overtly racist controversy in the British press.

This was ironic, because seaside architecture such as the De La Warr Pavilion was one of the few contexts in which uncompromisingly modern design was considered appropriate. Oliver Hill's magnificent Art Deco hotel at Morecambe (1932–3), Lancashire, with Marion Dorn carpets and sculpture by Eric Gill, was one instance of the acceptable face of the future; Joseph Emberton's masterly seafront at Blackpool was another.

Antagonism to modern architecture did start to diminish in the years leading up to World War II, if only on the principle that my enemy's enemy is my friend. In 1937 Berthold Lubetkin wrote that, in once-progressive Germany, "the flat roof has become the symbol of revolt, the mark of political unreliability; to design horizontal windows is to attract the attention of the secret police." And the Nazis' odious critique of

Owner. "Do TELL ME YOU *LOATHE IT."*

Bolsheviks, Jews, and their degenerate architecture led the British public to think that perhaps it wasn't so bad after all.

But it was too little, too late. Gropius had already left Britain for the more progressive climate of the United States; Mendelsohn followed in 1939, Chermayeff in 1940. Lubetkin, who gave up architecture after the war, provided Modernist British architecture of the 1930s with a poignant epitaph. "These buildings," he wrote in 1970, "cry for a world which has never come into existence."

HIGH AND OVER

AMYAS CONNELL FOR PROFESSOR BERNARD ASHMOLE, 1929–31

ABOVE Amyas Connell was one of the most exciting young architects at work in Britain between the wars. Buildings like High and Over attracted praise and blame in equal measure.

RIGHT Bernard Ashmole's living room, with lighting concealed behind ceiling panels, built-in furniture in jade-green cellulose with chrome trim, and armchairs designed by Connell.

I f anyone wants an illustration of just how thoroughly un-English the new architecture could be in the interwar years, High and Over is it. Even today, more than seventy years after it was finished, its hard, white angles and blind, staring windows startle the eye. This is exciting; it is architecture at its most provocative. But it is not what a house is supposed to look like. Not an *English* house, at any rate.

The client for whom High and Over was designed was as English as could be, and a man, moreover, who cared more than most about historical precedent. Essex-born Bernard Ashmole (1894–1988) was thirty-five years old when he decided to build himself a new house at Amersham, deep in the heart of commuter-belt Buckinghamshire. He was married with a young family, and had just been appointed Professor of Classical Archaeology at University College London.

An expert on numismatics and classical sculpture, Ashmole took up the chair at UCL in 1929, shortly after returning from three years as Director of the British School in Rome. It was while at UCL that he first met his architect, the brilliant young New Zealander Amyas Connell. Connell (1901–80) had served his articles in an architect's office in Wellington before working his passage to England as a ship's stoker in 1923, with his friend and fellow-student Basil Ward. Further studies at UCL led to his winning the Rome Scholarship in architecture in 1926, which is how he came to meet Ashmole.

ABOVE The house from the
southeast. Ashmole's
library is on the left, with
the master bedroom above;
the dining room and
kitchen are on the right,
and the glazed staircase
turret is in the middle.

Ashmole's choice of architect was courageous. Connell had built nothing of substance, his views were extremely progressive, and the designs he *had* produced were heavily influenced by Le Corbusier, whose work provoked rage, horror, and incomprehension among Britain's architectural establishment. (When Connell and Ward visited the Paris Exposition in 1925, see pages 46–9, it was Le Corbusier's Pavillon de l'Esprit Nouveau that excited them most.)

One of the most intriguing things about High and Over is its plan. As its name implies, the house stands high on a hill, overlooking the Misbourne valley. It is built in the shape of a Y, with three more or less equal arms radiating out at 120-degree angles from an hexagonal hall. One immediately thinks of those "ingenious devices" that the Elizabethans and Jacobeans loved so much, and the fantastic architectural alphabets dreamed up by Renaissance designers but never realized. Warmwell House in Dorset (c.1618) is one example of a seventeenth-century Y-shaped house in which three arms project from alternate faces of a central hexagon, and there are several others, including Newhouse at Whiteparish in Wiltshire (c.1619) and another Newhouse, this time in Herefordshire, which was built in 1636.

But High and Over is hardly a piece of Jacobethan pastiche, whatever its architectural precedents. Stark, flat-roofed, and clad in cement-rendered brick over a frame of reinforced concrete, it is carefully asymmetrical, despite its broadly symmetrical plan. The fenestration varies from one wing to another; an angular oriel projects out over Ashmole's library in the south wing, and a low, single-story extension containing domestic offices unbalances the northeast wing, which houses the dining room and kitchen. Most striking of all is the pair of flat concrete hoods or canopies supported on columns, which hover above the south and northwest blocks like giant aeroplane wings: despite the obvious associations with the machine age, they were intended primarily to provide shade and support for the Ashmole children's hammocks. The rest of the roof was taken up with an airy (and suitably remote) hexagonal day nursery, a night nursery, and nurse's bedroom. A lift brought meals up from the kitchen on the ground floor.

The three faces of the hexagon that don't connect to the living room, dining room, and library are still made to do some work. One houses the front door, of chrome-plated steel; the second opened onto a terrace that led in turn to formal gardens, which have since disappeared; and the third was

filled with a polygonal glass staircase that, on the rare occasions when the sun shone in Amersham, would let sunlight flood into the hall and the second-floor landing above. Four main bedrooms led off this landing: the master bedroom and dressing room were in the south wing, over the library, and included a built-in shower – quite a novelty in 1931.

The hall itself formed the most elegant interior in the whole house. In the center of a black marble floor inlaid with pieces of glass Connell sunk a glass basin, with a fountain that could shoot a stream of water as high as the first-floor gallery. This lit up at night. The sets of doors to the dining room, library, and living room – all capable of being folded back to create a single large space for entertaining – were made of steel and glass, and the inside surfaces of the glass were sprayed with translucent patterns of cellulose. All the main rooms had lighting concealed behind glass panels set into the ceilings, and decoration varied from plain orange walls in the dining room to chrome and jade-green cellulose in the living room, which also had a built-in wireless and – something of an anti-climax – several rather ordinary armchairs designed by Connell. Heating throughout the house was by means of radiators and built-in heating panels, although there was also an open fire in the living room.

High and Over was England's first real brush with International Modern, and England was not impressed. The local authority was reluctant to give planning permission, and only did so after a long battle. *Country Life* declared that "houses of this type ... can never fit into the English landscape in the same way as buildings constructed of local materials and in traditional styles"; and Sir Reginald Blomfield, a past president of the RIBA, asked very publicly what on earth was the point of the Rome Scholarship if Connell ended up "flouting the face of authority" in this way. Thankfully, Ashmole had vision enough to give Connell his head, and the result, which certainly flouts the face of authority and doesn't fit into the English landscape, is a delight.

ALDING

CONNELL & WARD FOR SIR ARTHUR LOWES DICKINSON, 1932

I n 1930, while High and Over (see pages 114–7) was still being built, Amyas Connell teamed up with his friend and fellow New Zealander Basil Ward, who was also his brother-in-law. Three years later they were joined by a talented young English architect, Colin Lucas, to form the firm of Connell, Ward & Lucas – perhaps the most exciting and controversial architectural practice in 1930s Britain. Unusually, the trio specialized in designing individual houses – often quite substantial – rather than the factories and public buildings favored by their more ideologically motivated contemporaries in the Modern movement. These ranged from the whimsical – for example, three concrete cubes overlooking the English Channel at Saltdean, Sussex, dating from 1934 – to the masterly, such as the curving expanses of glass in the house that Connell and Ward designed at Moor Park, Hertfordshire, in the early 1930s.

Soon after going into partnership with Ward, Connell was commissioned by Sir Arthur Lowes Dickinson to design a house at Grayswood, a picturesque Surrey village just outside Haslemere. After the furor caused by High and Over, Dickinson must have known what to expect when he approached Connell; and we in turn might expect that someone willing to bring the shock of the new into the redbrick, tile-hung rural Eden that was Surrey in the 1930s would be a movie mogul, a press baron, a thrusting young

ABOVE As this dramatic, sculptural chimneypiece demonstrates, Alding's builder was an enthusiast for futuristic and avant-garde interiors – not at all what one might expect from an elderly accountant like Sir Arthur Lowes Dickinson.

RIGHT Alding was renamed New Farm soon after it was completed. It provided just the kind of image to suit Crittall's advertisements.

CRITTALL WINDOWS

"NEW FARM," GRAYSWOOD, NEAR HASLEMERE, SURREY.
MESSRS. CONNELL & WARD, ARCHITECTS.

The windows are Crittall Standard "N" types, with a few of the same section made to special sizes. The "daylight walls" to the staircase are made of Standard reinforced Sash Sections. The windows are painted dark maroon-red and the walls of the house are tinted pale pink.

II 538.

ABOVE Seventy years after it
was built, Alding still
manages to surprise the
unwary visitor with its
angularity, its whiteness,
and its refusal to conform
to English ideas of what a
house should look like.

Jazz Age magnate. So it comes as a surprise to find that Dickinson was none of these things. He was a retired chartered accountant from another age, a man who had been born in 1859 and was the author of the textbook *Accounting Practice and Procedure*. A pillar of the establishment, he was on the board of governors of the London School of Economics and a director of a string of companies from the Ebbw Vale Steel, Iron and Coal Co. to Alvis Car & Engineering and Goodyear Tyres. It is refreshing to find someone of Dickinson's generation and background being prepared to build so uncompromisingly for the future rather than wallowing in the past.

Alding (now usually known as New Farm) proved just as astonishing as High and Over. Built of reinforced concrete – the walls were 10cm (4in) thick – and making extensive use of cantilever construction, it consisted of an L shape, with a staircase tower in the angle. Yet that scarcely does justice to the stunning visual impact of the house. From the entrance side it looks like a collection of white boxes of differing heights and sizes piled on top of one another. Narrow horizontal bands of window punctuate the plain walls, apparently at random; and rails around the roof give just a hint of the Liner Style. A cantilevered concrete canopy projects out over the entrance, raising slightly from the horizontal to disrupt – or perhaps merely to emphasize? – the right angles formed by the mass of cubes and rectangles. And the most prominent feature is the staircase turret, which is glazed on three sides, and cantilevered off a central column so that it seems to hang in space.

Sir Arthur Lowes Dickinson died in 1935, only three years after Alding was finished. The firm of Connell, Ward & Lucas broke up in 1939.

JOLDWYNDS

OLIVER HILL FOR WILFRED GREENE, 1930–3

Oliver Hill (1887–1968) was that rare thing, a British-born designer who embraced the new architecture with gusto during the 1930s. The son of a London manufacturer, he decided early on that he wanted to be an architect, and in the years leading up to World War I he followed a traditional Arts and Crafts route, learning his chosen trade in a builder's yard while studying form and color at the Victoria and Albert Museum in his spare time. After the war, in which he reached the rank of captain, he set about carving out a career for himself as a designer of country houses, either romantically thatched and picturesque or formal and neo-Georgian in the mold of Richard Norman Shaw, Reginald Blomfield, and Sir Edwin Lutyens. (Lutyens was a neighbor of Hill's parents in Queen Anne's Gate, London, and a family friend.)

In 1925 Hill went to the Paris Exposition (see pages 46–9). The experience hardly rated as a Damascene conversion, but his work began to show more and more affinities with Art Deco and Modernism, although never to the exclusion of traditional styles. It seemed as if he were eager to experiment but lacked the opportunity – and the necessary supportive client.

His chance to come out as a full-fledged Deco architect arrived in 1930, when a prosperous barrister, Wilfred Greene, and his wife Nancy

ABOVE Looking eastwards to
Joldwynds. Oliver Hill
created a pyramidal
collection of cubes and
curves that makes no
concessions at all to the
luxuriant Surrey landscape.

commissioned Hill to design for them a substantial eight-bedroomed weekend
retreat at Holmbury St Mary, about 16km (10 miles) southeast of Guildford
in Surrey. There was already a Victorian mansion on the site: Joldwynds was
a rather splendid thing surrounded by parkland, with gables and outrageously
tall chimneystacks. It had been built by Philip Webb in 1873. But it was too
big, too impractical, and too old-fashioned for the Greenes, and they decided
that it had to go. As Hill wrote a few years later, in the machine age "we
demand much more of our houses than mere charm of appearance."

The Joldwynds that replaced Webb's house was a gleaming monument,
one of the best Art Deco houses in Britain. Hill used brick for the new
building, but he rendered it with cement and carborundum, and then polished
it until the external walls shone like white marble. On the entrance façade,
which faced north, the effect was set off to perfection by a green copper door
flanked by gazelles and, as the notional pivot around which the dynamics of
the building revolved, a two-storied semi-circular staircase tower of glass. The
whole entrance front is effectively a single, sweeping curve, and the theme
was taken up by the staircase, by the circular drum on the roof (which held a
water tank), and by gently concave parapets.

The garden front was a little fussier. The Greenes wanted to make the
most of superb southerly views over the woods and farmland of the Weald,
and the main downstairs rooms – a big sitting room and a rather smaller
dining room opening onto a semi-circular loggia – look out in this direction.
Above these were the bedrooms, stepped back to give the Greenes and their

weekend guests individual sun terraces, each with separate external stairs leading directly down into the gardens. The metal casement windows were provided by Crittall; rather oddly, the architect opted for some windows to have vertical glazing bars, while others had horizontal bars.

Hill had a penchant for rich and exotic materials, something that caused his more ideologically correct contemporaries to view his work with suspicion. At Joldwynds he indulged himself to the full: the floor of the ivory-colored entrance hall was inlaid with coral and jade. This led into the sitting room, which was floored with Australian walnut and filled with furniture designed by Hill and made of white birch, eucalyptus, and Burmese padouk. The dining-room furniture was upholstered in white calf and veneered with ivory-colored shagreen.

Reactions to Joldwynds were mixed. The American textile and carpet designer Marian Dorn fell in love with it, declaring, "I would like to make a rug for that place more than anything I know of." By September 1934, when Christopher Hussey reviewed the house for *Country Life*, Dorn had done just that. Hussey was drawn to Hill's more conventionally picturesque houses, but, reluctant to appear a reactionary fogey, he contented himself with criticizing the uncertainty of the garden front of Joldwynds, with its receding planes and confusing mixture of verticals and horizontals, while admiring the "beautiful harmonies of curves" of the entrance façade.

BELOW The sweeping entrance front has a gentle, rhythmic quality. The copper door with its flanking gazelles assumes a secondary importance; the real focuses of attention are the curved staircase bay and the circular water tank above it.

ABOVE The white dining
room, with composition
floor, walls of combed
plaster, and furniture of
ivory shagreen and white
calf. The rectangular frame
holds a screen hiding the
serving table and the door
to the kitchens.

Sadly, the Greenes didn't share Dorn's enthusiasm, or even Hussey's cautious respect. Wilfred was cross about the cost of all those exotic woods and the poor quality of the building work. He complained to his architect that a piece of tar had fallen through a skylight and landed on his lavatory seat, "where it still remains" – until Hill came in person to remove it, presumably. He also criticized the oil central heating (supplied and installed by the West End firm of Hope's Heating and Lighting), which was spewing out fumes and smuts in equal measure. Nancy Greene confined her comments to the interiors, sending the architect a devastatingly detailed account of the "merits and demerits of the furniture which you designed for us." There were no merits: everything was too high, too hard, and too heavy. The end result was undeniably photogenic, she said; but "unfortunately Joldwynds was meant for a house to live in, not a lovely film set."

Joldwynds was finished in 1933. Three years later the Greenes turned to Berthold Lubetkin and Tecton (see pages 102–5) to repair their home, which was already losing its marble-like exterior finish. Lubetkin told them it would be cheaper to start from scratch, so they sold Joldwynds and commissioned him to build them a smaller, more conventional house in a corner of the grounds. Undeterred, Oliver Hill continued to design some brilliant Moderne architecture, notably the London Midland and Scottish Railway's hotel at Morecambe in Lancashire (1932–3), which was also beset with structural problems. After the war his highly individual Modernism was out of fashion, and he retired to a rambling manor house in the Cotswolds, where he entertained friends and wrote about the country houses of the seventeenth century. According to *The Dictionary of National Biography*, "he loved being out of doors, often without clothes, and kept many animals."

HIGH CROSS HOUSE

HOWE & LESCAZE FOR LEONARD AND DOROTHY ELMHIRST, 1931–2

The Philadelphia Savings Fund Society Building, in Philadelphia, was one of the twentieth century's most exciting architectural achievements. Completed in 1932 and around 140m (460ft) high, the thirty-six-story building was America's introduction to the International Style. And it earned its designers, the brilliant but short-lived partnership of George Howe (1886–1955) and the Swiss-born émigré William Lescaze (1896–1969), a place in the history books as the creators of the first truly modern skyscraper. Less well known is the fact that as the finishing touches were being put to the building, Howe and Lescaze were also making a wonderful, if rather unlikely, contribution to modern English architecture – a house for the headmaster of a private school at Dartington Hall, in the heart of rural Devon but only 16km (10 miles) from the sea.

ABOVE William Lescaze was well known for his ability to work within an uncompromisingly modern idiom. This made him a brave choice of architect for a small private school in the Devon countryside.

RIGHT A 1933 photograph showing the entrance hall of High Cross House. The walls were painted yellow, and the carpet was grey. "Clean, stark and beautiful," was Dorothy Elmhirst's verdict on the restoration of the six-hundred-year-old house that she and her husband, Leonard, had bought eight years earlier.

Dartington was the brainchild of Leonard Elmhirst and his American wife, Dorothy Whitney Straight. Both were radical thinkers, committed to the arts, education, and the idea of community; and both were convinced that if a rural estate could diversify and operate on scientific principles, it could still be a viable concern. In 1925 they bought the 400-hectare (1000-acre) Dartington Hall estate. The Hall was a picturesque but derelict fourteenth-century courtyard house, which the Elmhirsts immediately set about restoring with the help of William Weir, an architect who worked closely with the Society for the Preservation of Ancient Buildings.

As the Elmhirsts' vision of Dartington developed during the late 1920s, they started rural crafts – spinning, weaving, cider-making, and forestry. In 1929 they set up a junior school on the estate and, two years later, a senior school. The appropriate architectural setting might have plumbed the depths of quaintness; and indeed many of the first buildings were commissioned from architects who tended towards historicism and an attractive but folksy Arts and Crafts style. But shortly after plans for the senior school had been commissioned from the competent but uninspired British architect Oswald Milne, the Elmhirsts hired William Curry, a headmaster with clear ideas about how progressive education went hand in hand with progressive architecture. Curry needed some substantial accommodation. Moreover, he came to Dartington from Oak Lane Country Day School in Philadelphia, and

ABOVE High Cross House from the east, with the entrance front on the right. "At once I was filled with a desire to live and work in it," wrote a member of the Dartington teaching staff.

as it happened, this was a Modernist building with which Howe and Lescaze had made their name in 1929. Although the Elmhirsts were the nominal clients for High Cross House, as the headmaster's new house was called, they were happy to let Curry experiment. It was he and his wife Ena who were the driving forces behind the decision to employ the firm of Howe & Lescaze.

The brief given to the architects stated that "no effort should be made to copy the existing architectural style [of the Hall], since the house was to serve the needs of a modern family and should therefore, rather express the ideals of its inhabitants and also demonstrate the various forms of comfort which modern mechanical equipment provides." This "mechanical equipment" included an Aga stove, installed to make the servants' lives easier, and a radiogram fitted into the steps leading from the living room to the dining room. Rather more important was the deliberate asymmetry of the building, with projecting sun terraces, an off-center entrance, and, behind the double garage, a curving single-story study for Curry with separate access, so that pupils could come and go without disturbing the rest of the household.

High Cross House ranks with High and Over (see pages 114–7), Alding (see pages 118–9), and Joldwynds (see pages 120–3) as a pioneering piece of British Modernism. It was so modern that when Lescaze specified reinforced concrete, this proved too much for the local builders, and Robert Hening, the supervising architect on site, allowed them to use brick cavity walls and steel lintels. These were plastered. The Currys' part of the house was painted white, while the entrance front and the two ends were blue – a device that helped to counter a common criticism of Modernist architecture, its

BELOW One of the two roof terraces that Lescaze included in his design for High Cross House. This one is in the northwest part of the house, and was reached from the guest bedroom. The terrace in the southeast corner was for William Curry and his daughter.

ABOVE The living room, with curtains and furnishings in blue. The steps, which lead to the dining room, incorporated a built-in radio-gramophone. Steel furniture was supplied by Thonet of Paris.

uncompromising whiteness; although the fact that the blue was used to distinguish the servants' quarters and the guest wing leaves one wondering just how democratic it was. The interest in the psychological effects of color was carried through into the interiors, where Lescaze also deviated from the International Style's obsession with white. Walls were given graduated tints, with those closest to the light being plain white and those further away painted in steadily more prominent shades of grey or russet.

Metal played an important part in fixtures, fittings, and furnishings. Christopher Hussey, reviewing the house for *Country Life* in February 1933, eight months after William Curry moved in, noted the Crittall windows, the pressed-steel door frames, and a suite of steel dining-room chairs that he attributed to Mies van der Rohe.

High Cross House received a mixed reception. "The most miserable house I ever saw. All talk and no house," was Edwin Lutyens's predictable verdict. Curry was delighted with the design's serenity, clarity, and "a kind of openness," and suggested that such qualities "have important psychological effects upon the occupants." Lescaze, whose partnership with Howe broke up in 1934, went on to design more estate houses – less grand than High Cross, but still provocative in culturally conservative 1930s Britain. He also designed Blacklers, one of three boarding houses (1933); a gymnasium for the senior school (1934); and a central office and laboratory (1935). By the end of the decade Dartington had become a showcase for modern architecture, with the Lescaze buildings complemented by further work by Hening, who designed the other two boarding houses in 1934 and 1935 and collaborated with Gropius on the conversion of the old Hall's late-medieval barn into a theater.

In 1994 High Cross House, which had lain empty for some time, was restored. The striking blue exterior paintwork was reinstated, and the surviving furniture, including two Lescaze sofas and the suite of dining chairs (now thought to be by Serge Chermayeff rather than Mies van der Rohe), was put back in place. The house is open to the public.

BENTLEY WOOD

SERGE CHERMAYEFF FOR HIMSELF, 1935–9

A sensitive and contextual response to the natural environment is seldom a key element in avant-garde architecture of the 1920s and 1930s. Bentley Wood, a house designed for himself by the exceptional Serge Chermayeff (1900–96), is an exception.

After a colorful early career spent in South America, where he worked as a designer and tango dancer, Russian-born Chermayeff married into the Waring & Gillow furniture empire and in 1928 was appointed co-director of the Paris branch, along with the Deco *ensemblier* Paul Follot. During the three years he spent with Waring & Gillow he designed for the firm around sixty model rooms, in which he revealed a penchant for tubular steel, built-in furniture, and mirrored wall panels. He also created some classic Art Deco interiors including the scheme for London's Cambridge Theatre (1929–30), which had an auditorium in various shades of gold leaf and a dramatic Jazz Age foyer patterned in circles and semi-circles.

During the early 1930s Chermayeff worked as a freelance *ensemblier* in England, as well as working on BBC studios in London and Birmingham and designing wireless sets for Ekco. In 1931, during a tour of Europe, he made a pilgrimage to the Bauhaus at Dessau, where he met the German architect Erich Mendelsohn. Soon after the Nazis came to power in 1933, Mendelsohn left Germany and the two architects set up in practice in London. They produced a handful of outstanding buildings, of which the most famous is the De La Warr Pavilion (1933–5), an entertainment complex in Bexhill, East Sussex. This was the brainchild of the 9th Earl De La Warr, the seaside town's Socialist mayor, who asked the Royal Institute of British Architects to organize a competition to find the best design. But even before Chermayeff and Mendelsohn were proclaimed the winners in February 1934, the right-wing journal *Fascist Week* was condemning the RIBA for its "contemptible and despicable betrayal of our own countrymen" in encouraging "aliens."

While the controversy was raging, Chermayeff applied for planning permission to build a home for his young family at Halland, a hamlet about

ABOVE Despite being a British citizen and an Old Harrovian, Serge Chermayeff (shown here in the 1930s) was attacked in the right-wing press as a foreigner and an alien.

BELOW The local council took exception to the design of Bentley Wood, criticizing the plain cedar weatherboarding and the flat roof as being out of character with the surrounding countryside.

OPPOSITE The structural framework of Bentley Wood's garden façade was painted cream, and the raised terrace in front of it had a retaining wall of yellow brick. Chermayeff used different bonds to give a variety of textures.

32km (20 miles) northwest of Bexhill. Bentley Wood promised to be an inspired synthesis of traditional principles and modern design: spurning monolithic reinforced concrete, the architect opted for timber-frame construction and walls that were weatherboarded with Canadian red cedar. For the terrace on which the house stood, he specified buff-colored stock bricks; the same bricks were to be used for the garden walls. At the same time, this was no Lutyens-style Arts and Crafts cottage; it was a piece of unquestionably contemporary architecture, from the studied geometry of the south front, made almost entirely of glass and framed in cream-colored jarrah wood, to the double garage and the outdoor eating area, which was sheltered behind huge squares of partly-glazed trellis.

Britain's Town and Country Planning Act of 1932 had given new powers to local authorities, and Uckfield Rural District Council made full use of them. It turned down Chermayeff's scheme. Bentley Wood was compared in the local press to a chicken shed and a sanatorium, although the official grounds of objection were that the timber construction was inappropriate, and that "the flat roof is out of keeping with existing neighboring buildings."

This was breathtaking. There were no neighboring buildings, and the idea that timber-framing and weatherboarding were alien to Sussex defies logic. The real cause for concern, although the authority could hardly put it in writing, was Bentley Wood's modernity. Although local people were generally hostile, support for Chermayeff came from unlikely quarters, such as *Country Life*'s Christopher Hussey, who praised Bentley Wood as "so packed with ideas and … experiments that I venture to think it will continue

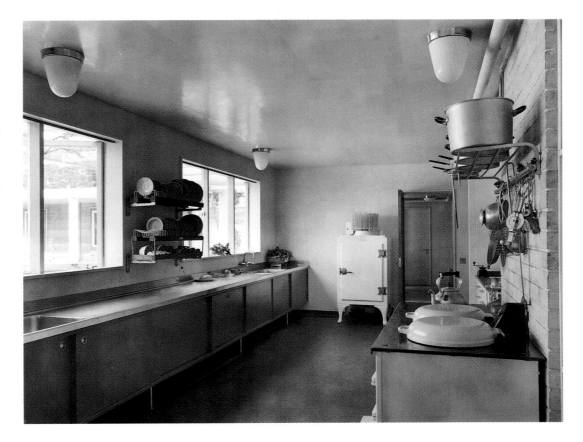

RIGHT The kitchen was equipped with stainless-steel sinks, a refrigerator, and an Aga stove. "And a very nice kitchen it is," commented *Country Life*: the magazine's reservations about modern architecture did not extend to modern conveniences such as these.

for some time to be a source of stimulus." The architect appealed against Uckfield's decision and after an angry public enquiry it was overturned.

Like the De La Warr Pavilion, Bentley Wood has become one of Britain's Modernist monuments. The plan is simple. The obsession with sunshine and outdoor life that lay at the heart of so much avant-garde architecture between the wars meant that all the interest was focused on the south front, which was separated from the entrance hall, kitchen, and a sitting room for the servants – even Modern-movement houses of the late 1930s made plenty of provision for servants – by a spine wall running from east to west. Beyond it, the study, living room, and dining room opened out of one another, while sliding windows allowed all three to open onto the terrace. (Ingeniously, Chermayeff carried the terrace paving into the house for several feet, further blurring the inside-outside split.) The decorative scheme was muted: the inner walls of the split-level study were laminated walnut; the living room was decked out in browns and greens, with abstract paintings by John Piper and Ben Nicholson at each end; and pride of place in the dining room went to an eleven-seater dining table of unstained birch with a blue linoleum top.

Upstairs the Chermayeffs' bedroom, which, with their own bathroom and dressing room, occupied the southwest corner, was veneered in elm. The children's nurseries were at the opposite end of the house, separated from their parents' room by two guest bedrooms, and soundproofed with cork.

Bentley Wood was finished by 1939, when it was reviewed by the *Architectural Journal.* Chermayeff emigrated to the USA in 1940.

ABOVE Sliding windows open onto the terrace from the living room, which occupied three of the six bays on the garden front. The other bays were taken up with the study (behind us in this photograph) and the dining room.

CHARTERS

ADIE & BUTTON FOR FRANK PARKINSON, 1938

Charters was built for Frank Parkinson (1887–1946). Born and raised in Guiseley, Yorkshire, Parkinson grew rich from heavy engineering. In 1936 he made three important decisions. The first was to donate £200,000 to Leeds University, where he had studied, for a new entrance and central block: the Parkinson Building was opened in 1951. The second was to marry Doris Burke, on whom he doted. And the third – remarkably in a decade that was busy lamenting the destruction of the English country house and the death of the leisured and civilized lifestyle that went with it – was to build a full-size stately home.

Forward-looking and progressive, Parkinson liked modern design and was determined to harness science in the cause of domestic efficiency. Indeed he did so to an extent rarely seen in English country houses of the period. At the same time he seems to have yearned for the life of the cultivated Georgian squire – farming and improving the land, entertaining like-minded friends, and surrounding himself with beautiful and elegant furniture and art-objects. As well as having the estate at Sunninghill, Berkshire, where Charters was to be built, he was a landowner on a large scale in neighboring Hampshire.

Doris Parkinson did not share her husband's enthusiasm for contemporary design. A choice between modern and antique interiors, between chrome,

BELOW View of the south front of Charters from across the park. The central group of five tall windows reinterprets an orthodox classical portico.

tubular steel, and built-in furniture on the one hand and Sheraton and Hepplewhite on the other, was, in her view, no choice at all. This dichotomy, the Parkinsons' vision of the country house as both a Corbusian machine for living in and the 1930s equivalent of Holkham or Kedleston stately homes, produced an aesthetic tension that pierced right to the heart of Charters. The house could never quite make up its mind what it was meant to be.

At first sight, however, there seems no doubt. Parkinson's architects were George Adie and Frederick C. Button. Their buildings, such as two in London, Athenaeum Court in Piccadilly (1936) and the Electroflo Factory in Acton (1937), tended towards an austere, rather stark Modernism with little or nothing in the way of ornament or decoration – although Button, at least, was well acquainted with the more flamboyant side of contemporary architecture, having previously worked for Wallis, Gilbert and Partners, the firm that produced Deco icons such as the demolished Firestone Factory in Brentford (1929) and the Hoover Building, Perivale (1932), both near London.

But Charters, which was finished in 1938, appeared to be frankly austere and uncompromisingly modern. Viewed from across the park, it was a gleaming white box. Narrow ground-floor windows emphasized verticality; above them there were expanses of white wall and horizontal bands of glass,

ABOVE Steps lead up to the south terrace, which forms a platform on which the house rests. The windows at the east end, which light the library and the main bedroom, continue around the corner of the building in Corbusian fashion.

uninterrupted as they traveled round the side of the building. The central section – the whole south façade, in fact – was dominated by five tall windows, nearly 7.5m (24ft) high, lurking behind projecting rectangular surrounds and, bizarrely, suggesting a car showroom. To the north, the façade breaks back deeply over the entrance to form a flat roof flanked by two pavilions, while this recessed section of wall above the door consists almost entirely of thick, translucent glass bricks – there for insulation, according to Parkinson, but it is hard to ignore the reference to Chareau and Bijvoët's Maison de Verre (see pages 154–7). To complete the impression of determined modernity, the flat roof was crowned with a massive wireless aerial.

But as one approaches the house, it becomes obvious that Charters is not all it should be. If it were serious about proclaiming the Brave New World of the future, its walls would be of reinforced concrete, or at least covered with a decent cement render. But it turns out to be faced with slabs of Portland stone – fine for St Paul's Cathedral or the British Museum, but not quite the thing for the futuristic palace of a vibrant entrepreneur in the 1930s.

The interiors are even more unsettling. Charters is a very big house, around 15m (50ft) deep and 60m (200ft) from end to end, with eight bedrooms, seven bathrooms, and an entire servants' wing, including a butler's pantry and a servants' hall. The plan is quite straightforward: a central single-story entrance hall leads into a spine corridor, and this in turn gives access to the reception rooms, all of which are on the south side of the house in order to make the most of the sunshine. A dining room and drawing room (to the west) and a boudoir and library (to the east) flank a huge two-story living hall, which is lit by those car-showroom windows that make such an impact across the park.

ABOVE The Great Hall. The decorative scheme was by the Parkinsons' *ensemblier*, Mrs. G.R. Mount, who also chose the furniture. The mural at the end of the hall was by Martin Battersby.

RIGHT Mrs. Parkinson's bathroom, lined in peach-pink marble and opulently functional, is notable for being one of the interiors at Charters that does not suffer from Good Taste and the cult of the antique.

ABOVE The morning room
was decorated in browns
and greens, with a cabinet
finished in Australian
walnut; the four paintings
that hung in the room (two
of which are seen here)
were the work of Adrian
Daintrey.

The visitor who shrugged off the Portland stone as an unfortunate but excusable façade might expect textiles by Marion Dorn, perhaps, and furniture by Chermayeff. At least a little glass and chrome, at least some white walls and abstract paintings. But they would have looked in vain. Doris Parkinson's ideas on interior decoration, and those of her *ensemblier*, Mrs. G.R. Mount, reigned supreme. The drawing room was panelled in pine, with geranium-red brocade curtains; the dining room was furnished with eighteenth-century chinoiserie chairs in mahogany and hand-painted Chinese paper on the walls; the decoration of Mrs. Parkinson's bedroom owed more to Louis XVI than to Lubetkin or Le Corbusier.

The technology was there, but it was well hidden. The curtains in the living hall were opened and closed by electric motors; the gas-fired boilers for the central heating and the thermostatically-controlled water heating were tucked away in the basement, along with the air-conditioning plant and the motors that drove the centralized vacuum-cleaning system. The chrome was to be found in the kitchens, where there were chromium-plated tiles and a combined electric dishwasher and waste-disposal unit, probably the only one in an English private house at that time. Only here and there above stairs – in the Deco opulence of Doris Parkinson's peach-pink marble bathroom, or the simple rectilinear forms of a bedroom fireplace – did contemporary design intrude on the tasteful, elegant, but hugely reactionary decorative scheme.

ENSEMBLIERS

Throughout the 1920s the most influential disseminators of both High and Low Deco were the *ensembliers*, the decorators and interior designers who offered a complete service to their wealthy clientele, providing everything from furniture and textiles to washbasins and ashtrays.

Some of the greatest *ensembliers* were men and women who had moved into interior decoration from very different backgrounds. Many had trained as architects, following in the tradition of English Arts and Crafts designers such as William Morris and Philip Webb: Robert Mallet-Stevens and Pierre Chareau both produced many schemes for interiors in the 1920s. Others were primarily craftsmen: the metalworker and lacquerist Jean Dunand, who, like Eileen Gray (see pages 68–9) – another furniture designer turned *ensemblier* – had studied lacquer before World War I with the Japanese master Sugawara, became absorbed in the business of interior decoration after the success of his work at the 1925 Paris Exposition (see pages 46–9). Jacques-Emile Ruhlmann, arguably the greatest and undoubtedly the most defiantly opulent of the French Deco *ensembliers*, was neither an architect nor a craftsman: he learned his trade in his father's upmarket painting and

BELOW This boudoir, designed in shocking pink by Gabriel Englinger and Suzanne Guiguichon, was one of the creations of the La Maîtrise atelier for the 1925 Paris Exposition.

RIGHT "Bobadilla" – a carpet design by Irish designer Eileen Gray. In the early 1920s Gray's Modernist flair made her gallery, Jean Désert, the talk of Paris.

decorating business in the early years of the century, moving from wallpapers and renovations to the type of expensive interior that provided Deco with its keynote – marble walls, ivory inlays, handmade papers, and dark wood veneers.

But it was the *grands magasins*, the department stores, that provided the Deco *ensembliers* with their greatest opportunities. The first was Le Printemps, whose Atelier Primavera was set up in 1913 by René Guilleré and his wife, Charlotte Chauchet-Guilleré. Others followed after World War I: the Galeries Lafayette began La Maîtrise in 1921, with Maurice Dufrêne as its director; the next year, Au Bon Marché opened its own atelier, Pomone, under Paul Follot; and in 1923 Le Louvre opened Studium, under the direction of Etienne Kohlmann.

Like a number of department-store ateliers, Kohlmann's Studium helped to introduce good design to a wide audience. But the work of the Paris *ensembliers* of the 1920s was fraught with conflicts that were tearing at the heart of European Art Deco – the tensions between the traditionalist and the modernist, between the socially committed left-winger and the capitalist who saw an inevitability in catering exclusively to rich plutocrats. In 1921 Dufrêne defended the elitism of La Maîtrise: "Decorators do not work for the 'rich' because they want to, or because they have no sense of social duty. They do so because they have no choice. In so far as he is an artist, the decorator can do what he likes. In so far as he is a businessman, he unfortunately has to do what he can."

The influence of the Paris *ensembliers* extended far beyond France. Pierre Chareau and Serge Chermayeff worked for the London firm of Waring & Gillow; so did Paul Follot, who left Au Bon Marché to head Waring & Gillow's Paris branch. In 1928 Jean Dunand created three interiors for the San Francisco penthouse apartment of the Union-Pacific Railroad heir Templeton Crocker. Atelier Primavera supplied items for W.J. Bassett-Lowke's New Ways (see pages 60–3) in 1926; and the whole idea of the *ensemblier* transferred happily to the United States, where designers such as Paul T. Frankl and Harriet E. Brewer carved out expensive niches for themselves, and London, where female society decorators Syrie Maugham, Sybil Colefax, and Nancy Lancaster made their reputations.

CITY SLICKERS

Hostility towards the city has been one of the moving forces in British culture ever since Keats declared that "To one who has been long in city pent,/'Tis very sweet to look into the fair/And open face of heaven." The countryside was purer, truer, better in every way. In *News from Nowhere* (1891), William Morris dreamed his utopian dreams of a return to a pre-industrial past in which the town played no part; and throughout the early twentieth century artist-craftsmen and their clients took their cue from him, deserting the city in droves in search of a lost Eden.

It is easy to forget, then, that a counterculture existed side by side with this anti-urbanism. In the decade between 1810 and 1820 the essayist William Hazlitt was of the opinion that "there is nothing good to be had in the country, or if there is, they will not let you have it"; and by the 1890s urbane and sophisticated young poets, swept up in the cult of the artificial, were declaring that real loveliness was to be found in the town, rather than in the hills and fields. "If any one sees no beauty in the effects of artificial light," wrote Arthur Symons in 1896, "in all the variable, most human, and yet most factitious town landscape, I can only pity him, and go on my own way." The Jazz Age generation of the 1920s, dominated by men whose experience of the countryside was the mud and trenches of warfare, agreed with him.

Right from the start, urbanism lay at the heart of Modernist and Deco architecture. This is not to claim that such architecture had no place in

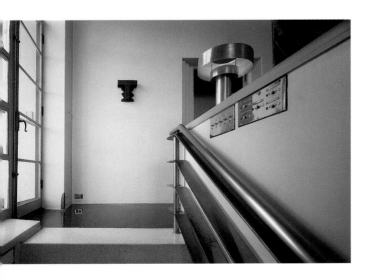

the countryside: as we have already seen, the individual house in the 1920s and 1930s was still more likely to be a country house than a town house or a suburban villa. But by "urbanisme" I mean a set of values rather than a setting; streamlining and sophistication rather than good, honest construction; concrete and steel rather than timber frames and thatch.

Modernity rather than tradition, in other words. And this is the key: the city was a fast, rapidly changing cultural construct. It moved with the times, and looked with mild contempt upon its conservative, reactionary country cousins. If change was what characterized the best architecture between the wars, then the excitement that went with change was more likely to be found in London, Paris, or New York than in villages, hamlets, and farmsteads.

Those who lived in the countryside viewed progressive architecture in much the same way as

PREVIOUS PAGE **The Del Rio House, Santa Monica, California, by Cedric Gibbons, 1931.**

ABOVE **Greta Garbo on Cedric Gibbons's set for the MGM 1929 movie *The Single Standard*. Hollywood was a powerful influence in establishing a link in the popular imagination between Art Deco and sophisticated living.**

LEFT **White walls and gleaming metal – the main staircase of the Del Rio House in Santa Monica, California, built in 1931.**

they did a Busby Berkeley musical. Both were entertainment. Both provided an escape from the tedious realities of everyday life. And both offered a tantalizing glimpse into a world that would always be beyond the reach of the vast majority of the population.

The houses discussed in this chapter are all responses to the city and the challenges it posed. Rudolph Schindler sought to bring his own notion of healthy rural living into the suburbs of West Hollywood, while Cedric Gibbons and Dolores Del Rio took Hollywood out to Santa Monica. At Eltham, in London, the Courtaulds and their team of architects and *ensembliers* imposed urban and urbane values on a medieval palace. On the other side of the city, in cosmopolitan Hampstead, Ernö Goldfinger's 2 Willow Road introduced a design for living that was both innovative and provocative; while in Montreal, Ernest Cormier showed how the lessons of the 1925 Paris Exposition could be put to use in a very different urban setting. The Maison de Verre, in the French capital, is the most exciting of all the buildings considered here, not least because Pierre Chareau and Bernard Bijvoët managed to disrupt our ideas of anonymity – so fundamental to city life – by creating a house of glass.

ABOVE Cedric Gibbons's set for *Our Dancing Daughters* (1928), one of the first films to introduce American audiences to modern European design.

BELOW A Streamline Moderne doorway on Sunset Boulevard, Los Angeles. For the modern-minded, Art Deco was ideally suited to urban life in the 1930s.

THE SCHINDLER HOUSE

RUDOLF SCHINDLER FOR HIMSELF, 1921–2

In the summer of 1911 Rudolph Schindler, a young student of architecture in Vienna, was staying in Austria's Styrian Alps. Sitting in a peasant cottage perched on top of a mountain pass and gazing out at the sky, he had an almost mystical revelation that the entire history of western architecture "was nothing but sculpture." Architects had been obsessed with carving and decorating and molding the forms that defined space. But they had failed to see that the real medium of architecture was space itself.

Back in Vienna, Schindler came across the Wasmuth portfolio of Frank Lloyd Wright's *Studies and Executed Buildings* and decided that "here was a man who had taken hold of this new medium. Here was 'space architecture'…. Here was the first architect." Like many Europeans, he was profoundly influenced by Wright's work, and in 1914, having graduated in architecture and engineering, he went to Chicago in search of the master. In 1917, after a three-year stint with a commercial architectural firm, he achieved his ambition and entered Wright's office. The experience of working

BELOW Space architecture – the Schindler House, on King's Road in suburban West Hollywood, is stark, organic, and an astonishingly innovative response to the needs of urban living in the twentieth century.

OPPOSITE The house was designed with two main residential units, one for the Schindlers and one for their friends the Chaces. There were no bedrooms in the conventional sense; the two families slept in open-air porches on the roof.

for Wright was important for Schindler's later development and helped to refine his ideas of "space architecture." But Wright, who was spending extended periods in Japan working on the Imperial Hotel in Tokyo, was not an easy man, and Schindler's four years in his practice weren't happy.

In 1920 Wright sent Schindler to Los Angeles to supervise the construction of Hollyhock House, the Mayan-inspired complex he had designed for the wealthy heiress Aline Barnsdall. Relations between Wright and Barnsdall were fraught, and the client grew ever angrier at her architect's apparent neglect of the project. Despite Schindler's best efforts, progress was slow, and in 1921 Barnsdall issued an ultimatum, saying that the house must be finished that summer. It wasn't, work stopped, and Wright was effectively dismissed. It was in the wake of this fiasco that Schindler, now married and in his mid-thirties, decided to settle in Los Angeles and set up his own office. His first independent commission – and his first real opportunity to put his ideas on "space architecture" into practice – was the house and studio he built on a suburban site in King's Road, West Hollywood. It was designed in 1921 as two residential units, one for himself and his wife Pauline, the other for his friends Clyde and Marian Chace. There was also a guest wing. A bank loan of $5000 and another of $3000 from Pauline's parents financed the project, which was completed in June 1922.

The King's Road complex was no ordinary apartment building. There was no living room or dining room; no bedrooms even – at least not in the conventional sense. Instead Schindler created five studios – one for each of the permanent occupants, and one for guests. They were arranged in three L shapes radiating from a central utility room (which was actually a combined kitchen and laundry that brought all the expensive domestic equipment together in one place for the use of both families), so that each L formed two sides of a patio or courtyard. The guest court was for services; the other two were integral to his vision of "space architecture" and the related ideal of healthy living and closeness to nature. Like the five studios, they were provided with hearths, and Schindler's hope was that the building should flow out into the open air, while the open air flowed in, to form an indivisible whole with the interiors, which he refused to define conventionally. The central metaphor was camping: occupants could cook their meals over open fires, sleep in the open air – the "bedrooms" were porches or "baskets" on the roof – and mix socially in the courtyards or withdraw to their own studios when they were working. Those studios broke down the traditional barriers between exterior and interior further by the use of sliding canvas panels which both separated them from, and joined them to, the courts.

The house-and-studio complex was built of redwood framing and concrete slabs, which sloped inwards as they rose and were separated by slender strips of glass to break up the monotony and create a rhythm of solids and voids. In line with Schindler's belief that architecture should be about space rather than sculpture, there were no decorated surfaces. The floor doubled as the concrete foundation, and the fireplaces were on the same horizontal plane, rather than being raised above or sunk below floor level. Revolutionary at the time, the house has since set the pattern for Californian living, giving birth to thousands of single-story dwellings that adopt flexible

BELOW Detail of Schindler's studio, with a view into the courtyard beyond. "Our rooms will descend close to the ground and the garden will become an integral part of the house," wrote the architect. "The distinction between indoors and outdoors will disappear."

responses to the functions of rooms within, and create a distinction between those rooms and the exterior space that surrounds them.

Like many an artistic community before and since, the King's Road complex foundered on the rocks of circumstance and personal differences. Clyde and Marian Chace left for Florida in 1924, and their place was taken the following year by Richard Neutra and his wife Dione. Neutra, who had known Schindler when they were both students in Vienna, joined Schindler's practice and remained at King's Road for five years. At first the arrangement worked well. The two couples had a similar outlook on life, and both had small children: the Schindlers' only child, Mark, had been born soon after the house was completed; Dione Neutra gave birth to Frank in 1924 and to Dion in 1926. For a time the house functioned as the setting for the healthy, outdoor, artistic life that Schindler had envisaged, with meals of fruit and vegetables taken in the open air, music and dance, and plenty of exercise.

But, as a result of imagined slights and professional jealousies, Neutra and Schindler grew apart, and they didn't socialize much after the first couple of years. The Neutras left in 1930. By now the Schindlers' marriage had broken down and Pauline had departed, taking Mark with her. In the mid-1930s she returned to King's Road – but not to her husband. She occupied the Chaces' part of the house; the connecting door to the communal kitchen was boarded up, and the couple never spoke, preferring to communicate by letter.

ABOVE Pauline Schindler's studio. The canvas panels on the left allow access to the grassed courtyard, which, like the studio itself, was provided with a fireplace so that the Schindlers and their young children could spend as much time as possible in the open air.

THE ERNEST CORMIER HOUSE

ERNEST CORMIER FOR HIMSELF, 1930–1

LEFT Like so many architects who were searching for a new style in the 1920s, Ernest Cormier found Art Deco and inspiration during a visit to the Exposition held in Paris in 1925.

BELOW The five-story house Cormier built for himself in Montreal makes use of its steeply sloping hillside site, and he opted to place the living accommodation on the two topmost floors.

G iven its geographical proximity to the United States and its strong cultural links with France, one might imagine that Quebec, and especially Montreal, embraced Art Deco with enthusiasm. In fact good Art Deco architecture was fairly thin on the ground there until the early 1930s; and, even then, it tended to be rather conservative, with little of the brio of Streamline Moderne or the elegance of Parisian High Deco.

There were exceptions, however, particularly when it came to Deco's own special building type, the movie house and theater. Joseph Alcide Chausée's Empress Theatre (1927), on Sherbrooke Street West, boasted a flamboyant façade plainly inspired by the Egyptomania that followed Carter's discovery of Tutankhamun's tomb in 1922. The interior was by Emmanuel Briffa, who also produced some pyrotechnic displays in the form of sunbursts and stained glass at the Château on Saint Denis Street (René Charbonneau, 1931), and an aggressively geometrical frieze and ceiling in the auditorium of the Snowdon on Decarie Boulevard (D.J. Crichton, 1936).

Less showy, but just as interesting, is the main pavilion of the Université de Montréal. Begun in 1924, but because of the Depression not completed for eighteen years, this was one of Montreal's first modern buildings. Built of reinforced concrete faced with yellow brick and dominated by a 75m (246ft) high central tower, it has a strong vertical emphasis, caused by narrow strips of window interspersed with shallow, projecting pilasters, which give the whole composition a stripped classical look. Many of the more public interior spaces use a combination of rich materials, such as black and colored marble, along with overtly "modern" features such as clusters of neon lighting.

The architect of the pavilion was Ernest Cormier (1885–1980), one of Montreal's most intriguing designers. The son of a Montreal doctor, he went to study in 1908 at the Ecole des Beaux-Arts in Paris (where he was taught furniture design by the *ensemblier* Ruhlmann) and remained in the city, working with Pierre Patout among others, until the end of World War I, except for two years at the British School in Rome. Around 1919 he returned home and set up in practice, but his early buildings showed little promise and little awareness of contemporary architectural developments in Europe.

Then came the Université de Montréal and, while its design was at a very early stage, a trip to the 1925 Paris Exposition (see pages 46–9), where he was impressed by Patout's Hôtel du Collectionneur. Edgar Brandt, whose iron

RIGHT In an inversion of conventional planning the staircase takes us down from the main entrance on the top floor. The story below is dominated by the library, with its golden columns.

gates had caused such a stir, was commissioned to make copper and brass doors and Deco standard lamps for the otherwise rather ordinary Montreal Courthouse Annex (1922–5) that Cormier was at that time working on with two collaborators, Charles Jewett Saxe and Louis August Amos, and some more metal doors for the Montreal Chamber of Commerce (1923–6), another collaboration, this time with Théodore Daoust. At the same time, Cormier's own architectural style, while never quite able to shrug off his "Bozart" roots, began to veer towards Deco.

This is why, when he came to design a house for himself on Pine Avenue West in Montreal, he chose Art Deco as the style. The five-story Maison Cormier, or Ernest Cormier House, which nestles into a steep hillside site falling away sharply to the south, was begun in 1930 and finished the following year. The northern entrance façade, which gives access to the fifth story, is obviously derived from Patout's Hôtel du Collectionneur: it has the same solid, blocky feel, the same deceptively simple angularity.

The front door is set back slightly, although the sense of mystery is accentuated by a projecting, semi-octagonal porch and its similarly shaped doorstep companion. Above the porch is a touching piece of egocentricity: Cormier placed a statuesque female figure with bobbed hair and a chic contemporary dress, who holds a model of the tower he was currently building at the Université de Montréal. A tall, narrow window to the right of the entrance is topped with three strips of stylized roses.

Inside the front door a corridor led past kitchen and cloakroom to reach a foyer, with a sweeping semi-circular staircase on the left, leading downwards; a dining room straight ahead; and a huge studio of 10.5m x 9m (35ft x 30ft) filling the right-hand half of the floor. The dining room was panelled throughout in walnut, and although undeniably opulent, it had, like so many Art Deco dining rooms, an air of boardroom formality.

Cormier had great respect for Ruhlmann: the fifth-floor staircase hall has one of the Frenchman's tables, which the architect bought at the Paris Exposition. His time studying with the *ensemblier* also shows in touches of luxury to be seen around the house: a serving table in the dining room of marble and macassar-ebony veneer; a studio floor in an elaborate pattern of intersecting circles of marble, terrazzo, and copper. The route from foyer and staircase to studio leads through two pairs of black marble-clad columns that are no more than cylinders, with neither bases nor capitals. But the most imposing interior is undoubtedly the library on the floor below. Built into the hillside, it has no windows and, like the studio above, its entrance is marked by four plain columns – but this time they are veneered in gold leaf. Visitors to the library must have felt as though they were entering the tomb of Tutankhamun.

Cormier lived in his mansion, which earned him a gold medal from the Royal Architectural Institute of Canada, for over forty years, and achieved a considerable local and national reputation as an architect. In 1975 he sold the house, which was at once classified as a historical monument by the Quebec authorities and carefully preserved, along with its furniture and interior decoration. It was bought in 1979 by the ex-prime minister of Canada, Pierre Trudeau, who used it as his Montreal residence until his death in 2000.

ABOVE A stone turret in the garden, reminiscent of the well at the Red House, designed by Philip Webb for William Morris and built in 1859–60, seems at odds with the modernistic feel that pervades the rest of the structure.

THE DEL RIO HOUSE

CEDRIC GIBBONS FOR DOLORES DEL RIO, 1931

When the movie producer David O. Selznick decided, in 1931, that RKO should make a South Seas romance, his requirements were simple. "I don't care what story you use," he told director King Vidor, "as long as we call it *Bird of Paradise* and Del Rio jumps into a flaming volcano at the finish."

Dolores Del Rio, whose Santa Monica house is a dramatic monument to West Coast Art Deco, was at the peak of her movie career at that time and one of Hollywood's hottest properties. Born in 1905 into an aristocratic Mexican family who lost their money in the Revolution, she had been married at sixteen and made into a star at twenty by her mentor and lover, Edwin Carewe (although her rise was helped by the fact that she was second cousin to the movie star Ramon Navarro). Carewe directed her in seven movies before their relationship broke up in 1929. Through films such as his *Ramona* and Raoul Walsh's *The Loves of Carmen* she came to epitomize a particular type of sultry Latin beauty, achieving the kind of box-office success that was extremely rare for a Mexican woman in the WASP-dominated Hollywood of the 1920s.

The Del Rio House, originally known as West Front, is often said to reflect the actress's love affair with the Moderne, which was certainly fast becoming the fashionable architectural style in Hollywood. But in reality the moving force behind the house and its decoration was her architect and husband, the MGM art director Cedric Gibbons, whom she met while making *The Trail of '98* for the studio in 1929 and married the following year.

Gibbons (1893–1960) came from a family of architects. He trained in the profession and worked briefly in his father's New York office before heading west in 1915 to work in the fledgling film industry. He is perhaps best

OPPOSITE The sleek lines and uncompromising modernity of the Del Rio House are perfectly in keeping with our idea of what a movie star's home should look like. In 1931, however, the design by Cedric Gibbons, Dolores Del Rio's husband, raised a few eyebrows.

ABOVE An asymmetrical stepped surround beckons one into the house. Gibbons made extensive use of "new" materials, including linoleum, chromium, and bakelite. The front door is faced with an alloy of stainless steel and copper.

LEFT Del Rio and Gibbons in the living room of their home in 1932. The moody, dramatic lighting creates the feeling that we have inadvertently wandered onto a film set.

BELOW The dining room reveals Gibbons's confident flair for the theatrical. The stepped arrangement of glazed lighting panels over the door tracks its way across the plain white ceiling, breaking up the box and subverting conventional notions of balance and proportion.

remembered today as the man who in 1927 designed a statuette to be presented at the annual awards of the newly formed Academy of Motion Picture Arts and Sciences (of which he was a founding member). Among film buffs Gibbons is also known for having the longest list of screen credits in cinema history – over 1500 in the course of a career with MGM that lasted thirty-two years. In fact he was not quite as prolific as the figures might suggest: when he went to work for the studio in 1924, he had the foresight to insert a clause in his contract stipulating that he should be credited with the art direction on every film that MGM produced. Nevertheless, as head of the art department, he was massively influential in forming contemporary American taste during the studio's heyday. And his own taste, exemplified in classics such as *Dynamite*, *The Kiss*, *The Thin Man*, and *Ninotchka*, was very definitely for the Moderne. Gibbons loved Art Deco, and he made sure that Depression America loved it too.

This passion extended beyond the movie set. Described in a 1931 fanzine as "modernistic in the extreme," the stark, angular lines of the house that Gibbons designed for his new wife proclaim his debt to Neutra, Le Corbusier, and the functionalists. But there is also an unmistakable air of theatricality about the building, a glorious and slightly quirky melodrama that reached a peak in the couple's sleeping arrangements: access from Gibbons's bedroom on the ground floor to Del Rio's on the floor above was by means of a ladder leading up to a secret trap door. A similar device was used by Pierre Chareau in the contemporaneous Maison de Verre (see pages 154–7), and it is possible that Gibbons, who kept up to date with the latest trends in European design, knew of the Paris house, which was attracting a great deal of attention in the architectural press at the time.

The entrance façade, which faces east, is austere and relatively uneventful. All the spectacle is concentrated on the west front, which looks out towards Santa Monica and the Pacific Ocean – hence the house's original name. There is a strong horizontal accent, emphasized by the collection of flat roofs, the projecting balcony (and its railings), the canopy above it, and the grids of glass that punctuate the wall spaces at irregular intervals. Gibbons also made use of the trick, so beloved of pure Modernists and Deco architects alike, of filling corners of the building with banks of windows in an effective reminder of the sophisticated structural opportunities offered in the Jazz Age.

The Del Rio House, however, has none of the sensuous curves found in, say, Burnham Beeches (see pages 26–7) or the Butler House (see pages 38–41). The sweeping decks and arcs of the Liner Style are missing: angles abound, and the straight line rules. Doorways are marked by surrounds of receding rectangles or by curious canopies that resemble inverted staircases, with the face of each "step" illuminated by electric lighting concealed behind translucent glass panels. The real staircase, which leads up to the main living room on the second floor, is a heady concoction of green terrazzo and chrome. Elsewhere, Gibbons uses plenty more opulent and exotic materials. There is bakelite and stainless steel, copper sheeting, black linoleum, and – most effective of all – huge expanses of mirror glass, which fill alcoves, decorative panels, and even whole walls. This gives a sense of space to rooms that are already fairly big, while adding value to the extensive concealed lighting. In truth, it also adds to the theatricality of the whole building, from the living room itself to Del Rio's dressing room, which is indeed that of a movie star.

Remaining in the ascendant during the early 1930s, Del Rio played the female lead in RKO's *Flying Down to Rio* in 1931, the film that brought Fred Astaire and Ginger Rogers together for the first time; and the next year saw her taking the title role in the historical drama *Madame Dubarry* and being choreographed by Busby Berkeley in *Wonder Bar*, a musical set in a Paris nightclub. But then came a spell in British second features, divorce from Gibbons in 1941, and a highly public affair with Orson Welles (with whom she made *Journey into Fear* in 1942). After separating from Welles she returned to Mexico, where her career took on a new lease of life.

Gibbons was not persuaded by his foray into architecture to give up his day job. He remained the head of MGM's art department until 1956, and he and his team won no fewer than eleven of the statuettes he had designed in 1927.

ABOVE With its huge mirror and banks of lights, Del Rio's sumptuous home dressing room conforms to the popular idea of a star's dressing room at a Hollywood studio of the era.

MAISON DE VERRE

CHAREAU & BIJVOËT FOR DR. JEAN DALSACE, 1927–32

Pierre Chareau's (1883–1950) association with the Dalsace family, which was to prove so important to his career as *ensemblier*, furniture designer, and architect, dated back to before World War I. In 1899 the young Chareau joined the Paris office of Waring & Gillow as a tracing draughtsman, where he met an Englishwoman, Dolly Dyte. The couple married five years later and, while Pierre worked at Waring & Gillow, Dolly gave English lessons. One of her students was Annie Bernheim. On the outbreak of war Chareau was conscripted into the army and, when he came out in 1919 and launched himself as an independent decorator, his first client was Annie, by now a close friend of the family and recently married to a doctor, Jean Dalsace. She and her husband commissioned Chareau to design interiors and furniture for their apartment on the Boulevard St. Germain. This in turn led to an invitation to decorate interiors for Annie's parents, including the Salon Chinois, a wonderful sitting room in bamboo and coromandel for

Madame Hélène Bernheim. By 1925 Chareau had opened his own shop, La Boutique, and was showing regularly at the Salon d'Automne.

At the 1925 Paris Exposition (see pages 46–9), where he gained acclaim for his contribution of the Ambassade Française to the Société des Artistes Décorateurs', Chareau met the Dutch architect Bernard Bijvoët (1889–1979), and the following year they collaborated on what was to be Chareau's first foray into building design, a golf clubhouse at Beauvallon in the south of France for Annie Dalsace's uncle, Emil Bernheim. White and angular, it contained an eclectic and utilitarian mix of Chareau-designed furniture, including folding metal chairs and bar stools of tubular steel. Then, in 1927, Jean Dalsace went to Chareau with a new project. The doctor owned an eighteenth-century town house in Paris, at 31 Rue Saint-Guillaume, and he wanted to demolish it and build a modern surgery and residence.

The Dalsaces' tastes were progressive and in line with Chareau's own, so the commission was exciting. But it was also challenging, not least because the top floor of the old house was tenanted and the tenant refused to budge. Assisted by Bijvoët, Chareau quickly hit on a novel solution. He simply propped up the upper story with steel pillars; then he demolished the lower floors and replaced them with the new house, leaving the tenanted story to perch on top of it. And from very early on in the design process, Chareau was determined that this new house should be a house of glass.

One can only speculate on his motives. There were precedents of a sort, but they came without any of the constraints imposed by the need for privacy. Burton and Turner's Palm House at Kew, of 1844–8, and the Crystal Palace,

ABOVE The duplex living room overlooks the entrance court. Vertical steel girders with exposed rivets are reminders of the method of construction.

BELOW Dr. Dalsace's rooms occupied the ground floor of the right-hand block of the L-shaped building. The family's living quarters were on the floor above.

RIGHT The main staircase leads to the living room from an entrance corridor, which gave access to Dr. Dalsace's workrooms and a waiting area for patients. The airy, insubstantial quality of the architecture is maintained in the light, open structure of the stair.

the 7.3 hectares (18 acres) of cast iron and glass designed by Joseph Paxton to house the 1851 Great Exhibition in London, are among the most famous examples. Apart from its novelty value, Chareau seems to have been influenced by contemporary concerns with a healthy environment: glass walls would both let in plenty of natural light and provide clean, dust-free surfaces.

Chareau and Bijvoët first experimented with the idea of creating a reinforced-concrete frame and using either clear or frosted glass as cladding. But they finally opted for steel columns, reinforced-concrete floors, and a membrane of translucent square glass bricks. The effect is astonishing. The entrance façade is set back about 10m (33ft) across a courtyard, and wraps around two sides of it in an L shape, with the long arm of the L facing the street. (The short arm contained service rooms, a kitchen, and a staff bedroom.) And what one sees is simply a vast grid of glass and steel, with the basic module a panel of twenty-four bricks arranged six high and four wide.

The ground floor housed Jean Dalsace's surgery, waiting area, and reception. His consulting room lay at the back of the building, giving access to the gardens, and was a double-height space that broke through into the second floor. This contained the family's main reception rooms, of which the most impressive was the living room, another double-height space overlooked by a landing-cum-gallery and lit by the wall looking out into the entrance court. Supporting steel girders were partially clad in black, but here and there sections of them were left exposed, as if to remind family and guests of their function. And the geometry of the grid was echoed and emphasized by the use of rubber tiles as flooring. These reappeared elsewhere in the house, although

Chareau also used black ceramic tiles, in Madame Dalsace's second-floor boudoir, for example, and in Dr. Dalsace's study.

A strange quality permeates the entire house, an intensely utilitarian functionalism that is slightly surreal in a domestic setting. And this surreal quality is accentuated by Chareau's choice of staircases. The stairs that led from Dr. Dalsace's ground-floor offices to the living room are open, without handrails and oriented towards the main glass wall, so that one ascends into the light; and the staircase from Annie Dalsace's boudoir to the master bedroom is not a staircase at all, but a retractable metal ladder. Louis Dalbet, a metalworker who had collaborated closely with Chareau since 1928, created much of the built-in furniture, and there were moveable partitions and screens, and walls formed from bookcases. The Dalsaces' son's bedroom had a metal bed fixed to the wall at one end with a hinged bar; the other end rested on a dais by the window, so that he could alter its position at will.

Work was well advanced on the Maison de Verre by the summer of 1928, and the frame was inserted that July, several weeks before Dalsace received the necessary planning permission from the city authorities. But it wasn't until four years and four million francs later that the house was completed and the Dalsaces were able to move in. They had been living nearby, though, and Annie was a frequent visitor to the site. So was Le Corbusier, apparently, for on several of Annie's trips to the Rue Saint-Guillaume she spotted the architect wandering around and peering at the building, which was destined to become one of the twentieth century's most famous houses.

BELOW **A gallery-corridor looks down onto the living room. Chareau installed built-in storage cabinets and bookcases along the corridor to create a screen between the two spaces.**

ELTHAM PALACE

SEELY & PAGET FOR STEPHEN AND VIRGINIA COURTAULD, 1933–7

"Clarification of purpose, the elimination of the inessential and disencumbrance from the pomposities of the past are the keynotes of the contemporary house," wrote the modernist architect Oliver Hill in 1939 (see pages 120–3). As a utilitarian fanfare for the future, this is an accurate reflection of the new Eden that avant-garde British architects were seeking, with increasing desperation, in the 1930s. But what if one wanted to combine an uncompromising modernity with the "pomposities of the past"? What if the "inessential" was also beautiful? This was the problem faced by Stephen Courtauld and his wife Virginia when they took on the Crown lease of Eltham Palace in 1933. Eltham had once been the residence of kings: a vast, moated complex where Edward IV had celebrated Christmas with 2000 guests, and Henry VIII walked in the allées and arbors with Catherine of Aragon. But it had never recovered after being stripped by Cromwell in the 1650s, and by the early twentieth century, with only the medieval Great Hall left, there were plans to surround it with a housing estate.

BELOW The fireplace in the dining room has ribbed and polished aluminium panels surrounded by Belgian marble inlaid with a Greek key pattern, a motif that recurs throughout the house.

Eltham Palace is only six miles from Westminster, and the Courtaulds were attracted by its illustrious pedigree, its proximity to central London, and the opportunity both to preserve a historic monument and, as keen gardeners, to create a spectacular garden in the grounds. There was no question of sweeping away Edward IV's Great Hall, which was in any case in the care of the Office of Works; but they had no intention of living in a ruin. They needed a comfortable, convenient house in the grounds of the Hall. The only decision was, what form should it take?

There were historicist precedents in contemporary English architecture – mock-medieval mutant monsters whose designers, in attempting to marry old and new, had failed to create convincing replicas of ancient buildings. There were also bolder efforts: in 1930 the Arts and Crafts architect Walter Godfrey had built a convincing house amid the ruins of Leybourne Castle, in Kent, with a convex gable end that formed one half of a medieval round tower.

The Courtaulds weren't prepared to go this far, and they opted for a middle-of-the-road solution that was both peculiar and peculiarly English. Their architects, John Seely and Paul Paget, produced a splayed U-plan, with Eltham's Great Hall as one arm of the U and a triangular entrance hall in the angle formed by the two wings. So far, so good. But they opted for a conservative Wrenaissance exterior for the new work, all red brick and stone dressings, which manages to be at odds with the medieval building without making a clear statement about the break with tradition. The Courtaulds were pleased, but public reaction was unfavorable.

ABOVE "An admirably designed but unfortunately sited cigarette factory" was *The Times*'s verdict on Seely & Paget's work at Eltham Palace. If only modern factories looked this good.

BELOW A dinner party at Eltham Palace in 1940. Ginie Courtauld can be seen on the extreme left; Stephen is at the far end of the table, just to the right of the lamp.

The heavy façade was neither modern enough for the Moderns, nor historicist enough for the architectural establishment. But if it wasn't entirely successful, the urbane and sophisticated interiors more than made up for these shortcomings. Stephen Courtauld was a reserved and deeply introspective character, the archetypal stiff-upper-lipped English gentleman. Ginie was an exotic: half Italian, half Hungarian, and a marchesa on account of a previous marriage to an Italian nobleman, she was lively, impulsive, and in touch with all the latest fashions. No doubt both Stephen and Ginie were responsible for the fact that Eltham was an ultra-modern home with electric fires, gas central-heating, internal telephones, a loudspeaker system to relay the sound of gramophone records around the house, and a centralized vacuum-cleaner system in the basement. But one suspects that the vitality and flamboyance of the interiors owed more to Ginie than to Stephen.

And what a joy those opulent interiors were – and are again, thanks to a recent restoration program by English Heritage, which took over the care of the house in 1995. The triangular entrance hall, a startling introduction to the house, was the work of the Swedish designer Rolf Engströmer, who also produced the blackbean and walnut furniture. This stood on a circular rug commissioned from Marion Dorn, whose bold, geometrically patterned carpets and textiles could be found in fashionable London interiors from the White

ABOVE AND RIGHT Designed by the Italian playboy and society decorator Peter Malacrida, Ginie Courtauld's bathroom (above) and bedroom (right) rank alongside the entrance hall as the finest interiors in the house. The atmosphere of controlled opulence in the bedroom, with its delicate marquetry panels, gives way to a gloriously self-indulgent display of gold and marble in the bathroom.

ABOVE View from the dining room, by Malacrida, through to the entrance hall. The applied lacquer birds and animals on the doors are by Narini, and were drawn from life at London Zoo.

Room in Syrie Maugham's Chelsea house to the lobby of Claridge's hotel. But the hall's two most spectacular features are the shallow glass dome that lights it; and the blackbean veneer that lines it, with marquetry panels by Engströmer's fellow countryman Jerk Werkmäster, depicting buildings in Italy and Scandinavia. The room is guarded by two larger-than-life marquetry figures, also by Werkmäster – a Roman soldier and a horned Viking bearing a halberd, who flank the glazed entrance doors.

There was no single *ensemblier* at work at Eltham Palace. Engströmer designed the hall; John Seely did the guest bedrooms, fitting them out with built-in, Liner Style laminated furniture. But if one had to identify an *ensemblier* who defined the Eltham look, it would undoubtedly be the Italian playboy and Mayfair decorator Peter Malacrida, who was responsible for the drawing room, dining room, library, and Ginie's bedroom suite. The drawing room, which boasted antique rugs, cream walls, and garishly painted faux ceiling timbers, is perhaps his least successful creation; although he more than made up for it with the mahogany-lined library and the Deco dining room, all black marble and ebonized woods inlaid with bold, geometrical patterns, and a ceiling of shining aluminium leaf. Malacrida's masterpiece is Ginie's suite. Her oval bedroom is lined with pale maple punctuated with sycamore pilasters, like some shrine to an ancient goddess, and curved doorways inlaid with marquetry open onto the first-floor landing and the goddess's inner sanctum, a bathroom lined with onyx and gold mosaic.

2 WILLOW ROAD

ERNÖ GOLDFINGER FOR HIMSELF, 1937–9

Ernö Goldfinger's Willow Road development was not popular in London's fashionable Hampstead. When the design was submitted to Hampstead Borough Council in 1937, it had already been pared down from a block of flats to a row of four houses and finally to a terrace of three – No. 1 owned by the Goldfingers and rented out, No. 2 their own residence, and No. 3 pre-sold and finished to the client's own designs. But it still made the national press. Conservative conservation-minded locals were appalled at the prospect of a Modernist horror on their doorstep. The Hampstead Heath and Old Hampstead Protection Society, and in particular their Secretary, future Home Secretary Henry Brooke, declared that the new terrace would be "disastrously out of keeping" with the neighborhood.

In countering that the three houses were designed as a modern adaptation of a Georgian terrace, Goldfinger was supported by influential neighbors. But his arguments were entirely specious. Willow Road *was* out of keeping with the houses that surrounded it, and it bore not the faintest resemblance to a Georgian terrace (although the architect's radical attempt to reinterpret the terrace form is one of the most exciting features of the design). But Hampstead needed a kick in the pants to propel it into the twentieth century,

and, in all fairness, Brooke and his friends failed to understand that the Willow Road terrace was not to be a concrete Corbusian box.

For Goldfinger, as for so many architects in the years between the wars, Modernism was an article of faith. But there is an absence of sentimentality in his buildings, a heartlessness that ushered in the New Brutalism of the post-war years and ushered out the sneaking fascination with ornament that had kept Art Deco alive as a style, or at least as a tendency, throughout the 1930s. There is also something slightly chilling in his pronouncements on the three elements of modern architecture: "the permanent structure; the much less permanent services; and an even more fleeting component, the human requirements." Something chilling, too, considering the left-wing principles he espoused in his private life, in his willingness to work with property developers, and his contempt for idealistic colleagues.

And that is rather a pity, because the Ernö Goldfinger who struggled to establish himself as an architect in Paris and London was nowhere near as humorless or soulless as this. Born of well-to-do parents in Budapest in 1902, he moved to Paris to study when he was eighteen. A mandatory spell at the Ecole des Beaux-Arts was followed by an equally mandatory sense of frustration with his conservative teachers, and in 1925 he joined with other young radicals in asking Le Corbusier to open a new atelier. The Swiss master

ABOVE The dining room has a deep window sill, which gradually became filled with ornaments over the years. The dining table, with its linoleum top, was originally made for the apartment in Highpoint I, not far away in Highgate, into which the Goldfingers and their young son moved in 1935.

refused, suggesting instead that they approach his own teacher, Auguste Perret, whose experiments with reinforced-concrete structures had made him something of an icon in avant-garde architectural circles. Goldfinger absorbed Perret's interest in classical simplicity and clean lines, and throughout his life his own work exhibited an extreme austerity.

In 1933, in Paris, Goldfinger married Ursula Blackwell, an English girl with a wealthy background in Crosse & Blackwell soups, and the following year he set up in practice in London. Architectural commissions were slow in coming, and when a site became available in Willow Road, the couple saw an opportunity both to advertise Ernö's talents and to invest some of Ursula's money. Despite all the local objections, they eventually managed to obtain planning consent to build their three houses, partly because of the architect's argument that he was reinterpreting the idea of the Regency streetscape, and partly because the objectors came to realize that, although the block made extensive use of concrete for floor slabs, stairs, inner walls, and supporting columns, Goldfinger was not going to allow this to show, choosing instead to clad the concrete frame with an exterior brick skin.

The ground floor of No. 2 is taken up with garage, service areas, and an entrance lobby. A spiral staircase with a banister of rope balusters and a brass handrail leads up to the main living rooms – a conscious echo of Georgian planning, and perhaps a reference to Le Corbusier's tendency to provide second-floor living spaces in his houses. Goldfinger made extensive use of folding partitions to maximize the flexibility of this part of the house. There is a dining room, a studio, a living room, and a study, all grouped around the central stair; but the dining room can be combined with the studio, and the studio with the living room. The partitions were treated differently: that separating the studio from the living room, for example, is faced in mahogany on one side and oak on the other. Today the study contains many of Ernö's books, including *Goldfinger* (the architect's name is reputed to have inspired that of Ian Fleming's most notorious villain); and Auguste Perret's top hat.

The top floor of the house contained the Goldfingers' bedroom, with connecting bathroom and lavatory; the nurseries; and a guest room, which, as their son Peter recalled, was constantly occupied by visitors who ranged from "near and distant relatives to a Swiss banker and a young female Italian film director." The house was not completed until the summer of 1939, a few weeks before the outbreak of World War II, and the couple were active in raising funds for various anti-Nazi good causes.

The war meant that Willow Road was never quite the advertisement that the Goldfingers intended. If it had been, and Ernö had built more terraces on the same human scale, his place in history would have been assured. But his subsequent work, especially the harsh residential tower blocks he built for the Greater London Council in the 1960s and 1970s, have made him an architect that people love to hate, one of the many unacceptable faces of Modernism. This is unfortunate, because, as anyone who visits Willow Road today will see, his understanding of domestic architecture in the twentieth century was comprehensive and appealing.

LEFT The ground-floor entrance hall, with its grid of obscured glass; a letterbox is set into one of the panes. The chair, made of bent plywood, is a prototype for one of Goldfinger's most famous furniture designs.

TRANSPORTS
OF DELIGHT

In the years between the two world wars, Art Deco designers of all kinds, from architects and *ensembliers* to metalworkers and graphic artists, were fascinated with the idea of speed and movement. So too were their clients. Fast cars and fast women are among the most enduring images of the Jazz Age, an age in which Lindbergh flew the Atlantic, Malcolm Campbell broke the land speed record nine times, and the *Flying Scotsman* roared up the railway track between London and Edinburgh at 160kmph (100mph).

There was a new aesthetics of speed during the 1920s and 1930s, and many of the architects mentioned in this book helped to forge it. In 1931 Norman Bel Geddes (see pages 20–1) patented a

design for a streamlined locomotive. (He also patented ideas for teardrop-shaped automobiles, buses, yachts, and airplanes.) Eckart Muthesius (see pages 28–9) designed the passenger cabin of the Maharajah of Indore's luxury airplane, with rather fetching sunburst designs on the leather seats; René Lalique created an interior for the French presidential sleeping car. Architects were also inspired to produce streamlined transport architecture – airports, rail terminals, car showrooms. Robert Mallet-Stevens (see pages 86–9) designed filling stations for Alfa Romeo; Walter Dorwin Teague also designed filling stations, for Texaco, as well as producing streamlined automobiles, notably the 1932 Mammon 16.

One reason for Art Deco's love affair with trains, boats, airplanes, and cars is that they provided a potent metaphor for escape, for traveling hopefully and hedonistically, for leaving all one's worries behind. Another, oddly enough, is the link between the Arts and the Crafts forged half a century before in Britain by William Morris. In the wake of Morris's determination to reunite artist and craftsman, it was now entirely appropriate for the industrial designer to consider aesthetics, and for the architect to trespass into the field of industrial design. And most obvious of all, perhaps, is the fact that by the 1920s industrialization had produced its own aesthetic; the well-designed machine had become a yardstick by which everything else had to be judged. As Sheldon Cheney wrote in *The New World Architecture* (1930), a house should be more like a car "that has just the combination of mechanical efficiency and comfort, of cleanliness and pleasurable brightness, of mechanically perfect shelter and of beauty out of proportioning and structure, that we should relish in a house."

RIGHT In the Jazz Age, speed, sophistication, and hard liquor made a seductive combination, and the designer of this poster advertising the London and North Eastern Railway's London-to-Edinburgh service took full advantage of the fact.

The most magnificent synthesis of speed and style that Deco ever produced was the Compagnie Générale Transatlantique's *Normandie*. This 80,550-tonne (79,280 tons) ocean liner, which made its maiden voyage from Le Havre to New York in May 1935, was built to a revolutionary design that two years later enabled it to capture the Blue Riband for a record-breaking transatlantic crossing time of three days, twenty-two hours, and seven minutes. But speed wasn't the only imperative: CGT set new standards in luxury and comfort with *Normandie*, and turned to the best French designers for help. The vessel was illuminated by lamps and chandeliers designed by René Lalique. The lacquerist Jean Dunand, who had created a smoking room for the Ambassade Française at the 1925 Exposition, (see pages 46–9) designed another for the *Normandie*. CGT brought in France's best *ensembliers* to decorate the first-class state rooms, among them Louis Süe, who, with his partner in La Compagnie des Arts Français, André Mare, had already designed the *grand salon* on CGT's sister ship, the *Ile-de-France*.

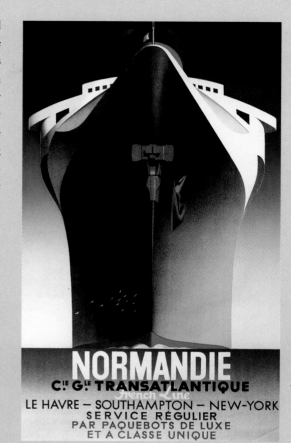

LEFT For his famous poster advertising CGT's new, luxurious transatlantic liner, Cassandre chose a very low angle of sight to emphasize the vessel's massive bulk and streamlined bow.

LEFT One of the luxury state rooms on the *Normandie*. Many of the best Art Deco designers contributed to the interiors of the "ship of light," including Lalique, Dunand, and Louis Süe.

BIBLIOGRAPHY

Abercrombie, Patrick, ed: *The Book of the Modern House – a Panoramic Survey of Contemporary Domestic Design* (Waverley, 1939)

Allan, John: *Berthold Lubetkin – Architecture and the Tradition of Progress* (RIBA Publications, 1992)

Arwas, Victor: *Art Deco* (Abrams, 1980)

Aslet, Clive: *The Last Country Houses* (Yale University Press, 1982)

Banham, Reyner: *Theory and Design in the First Machine Age* (Architectural Press, 1960)

Bayer, Patricia: *Art Deco Interiors* (Thames & Hudson, 1990)

Bayer, Patricia: *Art Deco Architecture* (Thames & Hudson, 1992)

Bel Geddes, Norman: *Horizons* (Little, Brown & Co, 1932)

Benton, Tim: *The Villas of Le Corbusier, 1920-1930* (Yale University Press, 1987)

Blomfield, Reginald: *Modernismus* (Macmillan, 1934)

Boesiger, W, ed: *Richard Neutra – Buildings and Projects* (Thames & Hudson, 3 vols, 1964-66)

Brunhammer, Yvonne: *Le Style 1925* (Payot, 1987)

'Burnham Beeches', *The Australian Home Beautiful*, 1 March 1934 (pp3-13)

Camard, Florence: *Ruhlmann – Master of Art Deco* (Abrams, 1984)

Cantacuzino, Sherban: *Wells Coates – a Monograph* (Gordon Fraser Gallery, 1978)

Capitman, Barbara Baer: *Deco Delights – Preserving the Beauty and Joy of Miami Beach Architecture* (E.P. Dutton, 1988)

Cheney, Sheldon: *The New World Architecture* (Longmans, Green & Co, 1930)

Cohen-Rose, Sandra: *Northern Deco – Art Deco Architecture in Montreal* (Corona, 1996)

Dean, David: *The Thirties – Recalling the English Architectural Scene* (Trefoil Books, 1983)

Druesedow, Jean L: *Authentic Art Deco Interiors and Furniture* (Dover, 1997)

Dufrène Maurice: *Authentic Art Deco Interiors from the 1925 Paris Exhibition* (Antique Collectors' Club, 1989)

Duncan, Alastair: *Art Deco Furniture* (Thames & Hudson, 1992)

Elwall, Robert: *Ernö Goldfinger* (Academy Editions, 1996)

Fellows, Richard A: *Sir Reginald Blomfield – An Edwardian Architect* (Zwemmer, 1985)

Ford, James and Katherine Morrow Ford: *Classic Modern Homes of the Thirties* (Dover, 1989)

Friedman, Mildred: *De Stijl, 1917–1931 – Visions of Utopia* (Phaidon, 1982)

Gebhard, David and Harriette von Breton: *Los Angeles in the Thirties, 1931-1941* (2nd edn, Hennessey & Ingalls, 1989)

Giraud, Maggie, ed: *House for Mr Curry* (Dartington Hall Trust, 2000)

Hillier, Bevis: *Art Deco of the 20s and 30s* (Studio Vista, 1968)

Hillier, Bevis: *The World of Art Deco* (Studio Vista, 1971)

'House for Earl Butler, Des Moines, Iowa', *Architectural Forum*, September 1937 (pp179-186)

'House near Halland, Sussex – Serge Chermayeff, Architect', *Architectural Review* (pp63-78)

Hussey, Christopher: 'A Modern Country House – Bentley, near Halland, Sussex', *Country Life*, 26 October and 2 November 1940 (pp368-71, 390-3)

Hussey, Christopher: 'Charters, Sunningdale, Berkshire', *Country Life*, 24 November, 1 and 8 December 1944 (pp904-7, 948-51, 992-5)

Hussey, Christopher: 'Eltham Palace', *Country Life*, 15, 22, 29 May 1937 (pp534-9, 568-73, 594-99)

Hussey, Christopher: 'High and Over, Amersham, Bucks', *Country Life*, 19 September 1931 (pp302-7)

Hussey, Christopher: 'High Cross House', *Country Life*, 11 February 1933 (pp144-9)

Hussey, Christopher: 'Joldwynds', *Country Life*, 15 September 1934 (pp276-281)

Jeanneau, Hubert and Dominique Deshoulières: *Rob Mallet-Stevens: Architecte* (Archives d'architecture moderne, 1980)

Le Corbusier: *Towards a New Architecture* (Architectural Press, 1927)

Lustenberger, Kurt: *Adolf Loos* (Artemis, 1994)

March, Lionel and Judith Sheine, eds: *R M Schindler – Composition and Construction* (Academy Editions, 1993)

McGregor, Robert: *The Art Deco City – Napier, New Zealand* (Art Deco Trust, 1998)

Moffat, Alistair, ed: *Remembering Charles Rennie Mackintosh* (Colin Baxter Photography, 1989)

Niggl, Reto: *Eckart Muthesius – India 1930–1939* (Goethe-Institut, 1999)

'The Paris Exhibition MDCCCCXXV', *Architectural Review* [special issue], July 1925

Pevsner, Nikolaus: *Pioneers of the Modern Movement from William Morris to Walter Gropius* (Faber & Faber, 1936)

Powers, Alan: *2 Willow Road, Hampstead* (National Trust, 1996)

'Recent English Domestic Architecture', *Architectural Review*, December 1928 (pp233-336)

Richards, J.M.: *An Introduction to Modern Architecture* (Penguin, 1940)

Rothery, Sean: *Ireland and the New Architecture, 1900–1940* (Lilliput Press, 1991)

Sharp, Dennis: *Twentieth-century Architecture – a Visual History* (Lund Humphries, 1991)

'Silhouette': 'New Ways', *Architectural Review*, November 1926 (pp175-9)

Sparke, Penny: *A Century of Design – Design Pioneers of the 20th Century* (Mitchell Beazley, 1998)

Taylor, Brian Brace: *Pierre Chareau, Designer and Architect* (Benedikt Taschen, 1992)

Teague, Walter Dorwin: *Design This Day – the Technique of Order in the Machine Age* (Harcourt, Brace & Co, 1940)

Turner, Michael: *Eltham Palace* (English Heritage, 1999)

van Doesburg, Theo : *On European Architecture – Complete Essays from Het Bouwbedrijf 1924-1931* (Birkhäuser Verlag, 1990)

Warncke, Carsten-Peter: *The Ideal as Art – De Stijl 1917–1931* (Benedikt Taschen, 1991)

Waugh, Evelyn: *Decline and Fall* (Chapman & Hall, 1928)

Windsor, Alan: *Peter Behrens – Architect and Designer* (Architectural Press, 1981)

INDEX

ACKNOWLEDGMENTS

PUBLISHERS ACKNOWLEDGMENTS
The publishers would like to thank the following people who kindly provided photographs for this book:

Front cover ©2001 Dan Forer/Crescent Suites Hotel @ Hilton Grand, 1430 Ocean Drive, Miami Beach, FL 33139, telephone number 001 305 604 8225; back cover, left K.N. Integer; back cover, right Ray Main/Mainstream/Eltham Palace; back flap Octopus Publishing Group Ltd/Carlo Chinca.

Endpapers Angelo Hornak/Courtesy the Victoria & Albert Museum; 1 Jean-Loup Charmet; 2 Arcaid/Richard Bryant; 4 Corbis UK Ltd/Angelo Hornak; 6 Corbis UK Ltd/Gianni Dagli Orti; 7 top by permission of the Dartington Hall Trust; 7 bottom Bridgeman Art Library/Victoria & Albert Museum, London; 8 bottom left ©2002 Michael Freeman; 8 bottom right Architectural Association Picture Library/Julian Feary; 9 left Bridgeman Art Library/Egyptian National Museum, Cairo/Giraudon; 9 right Norma Evenson; 10 left AKG, London; 10 right Jean-Loup Charmet; 11 Archives d'Architecture Moderne, Bruxelles; 12 top Advertising Archives; 12 bottom Dover Publications, Inc; 13 Art Blume SL/© photograph Pepe Navarro; 14 left and right The Art Archive; 15 Arcaid/Nick Dawe; 16 and 17 K N Integer; 18 left The Art Archive/Nicolas Sapieha; 18 right Bridgeman Art Library/Collection Hervé, Paris; 19 top Corbis UK Ltd/Underwood & Underwood; 19 bottom Brent Meersman (Chairman, Cape Art Deco Society); 20 top and bottom The Norman Bel Geddes Collection, The Performing Arts Collection, Harry Ransom Humanities Research Center, The University of Texas at Austin, by permission of Edith Lutyens Bel Geddes, Executrix; 21 British Library Newspaper Library; 22 AKG, London/Reinhard Friedrich, Berlin; 23, 24, 25 Stiftung Archiv der Akademie der Künste, Berlin/Hans-Scharoun Archiv; 26 bottom The Australian Tourist Commission; 27 top and bottom State Library of Victoria; 28 top and bottom Eckhard Muthesius in India 1930-1939, Architecture, Design, Photography, Goethe Institut exhibition with accompanying publication by Dr Reto Niggl; 30 top Corbis UK Ltd/Bettmann Archive; 30 bottom, 31, 32, 33 Paul Rocheleau; 34 top and bottom, 35, 36-37 NZ House & Garden/Paul McCredie; 38 Schnectady Museum; 38-39 bottom Randy Juster; 39 and 40 top Schnectady Museum; 40 bottom Chicago Historical Society/Hedrich Blessing Collection; 41 Schnectady Museum; 42 top Scott Tallon Walker Architects/John Donat Photography; 42 bottom, 43 Irish Architectural Archive, 44, 45 Irish Architectural Archive; 46 Roger-Viollet/Harlingue-Viollet; 47 top and bottom Jean-Loup Charmet/Bibliothèque des Arts Décoratifs, Paris; 48 Jean-Loup Charmet/Henri Manuel; 49 top The Art Archive; 49 bottom Roger-Viollet/Branger-Viollet; 50-51 Arcaid/Raul Raftery; 52 Arcaid/Richard Bryant; 52-53 Archives d'Architecture Moderne, Bruxelles; 53 The Art Archive; 54, 55 top right, 55 bottom left, 56, 57 top and bottom, 58, 59 Frank den Oudsten, Amsterdam; 60 Architectural Press; 61 top right AKG, London; 62 and 63 Northamptonshire Record Office; 64 Julius Shulman; 65 top © 2002 Michael Freeman; 65 bottom and 66 Julius Shulman; 67 © 2002 Michael Freeman; 68, 69 left, 69 right RIBA Library Photographs Collection, London; 70 top left AKG, London/Paul Almasy; 70 bottom right Arcaid/David Churchill, 71, 72, 73 Arcaid/Paul Raftery;

74 Arcaid/Martin Jones; 75 Arcaid/Paul Raftery; 76 The Art Archive/Musée des Arts Décoratifs, Paris, 76 bottom left Christie's Images; 77 left The Art Archive/Musée des Décoratifs Paris; 77 right Sotheby's Picture Library; 78-79 Corbis UK Ltd/Joseph Sohm, Visions of America; 80 top AKG, London/Paul W John; 80 bottom Randy Juster; 81 top Corbis UK Ltd/Bettmann; 81 bottom Avery Architectural and Fine Arts Library, Columbia University in the City of New York; 82 top and bottom Frank den Oudsten, Amsterdam; 83 KLM Aerocarto - Arnhem, Holland; 84, 85 Frank den Oudsten, Amsterdam; 87 Arcaid/Paul Raftery; 88, 89 Archives d'Architecture Moderne, Bruxelles; 90 top left National Portrait Gallery, London; 90, 91 Sarah Jackson; 92, 93, 94, 95 Patricia Bayer; 96, 97, 98, 99 New Zealand Art Deco Society; 100 left University of East Anglia Archive (Pritchard Papers); 100 right, 101, 102 top and bottom RIBA Library Photographs Collection, London; 103, 104 Arcaid/Lewis Gasson; 105 RIBA Library Photographs Collection, London; 106 top and bottom, 107 Julius Shulman; 108, 109 top and bottom courtesy Dallas Historical Society; 110-111, 112 left Arcaid/Nick Dawe; 112 right Blackpool Pleasure Beach; 113 top Arcaid/Richard Bryant; 113 bottom Punch Cartoon Library; 114 top Book Art & Architecture Picture Library; 114 bottom, 115, 116 left Country Life Picture Library; 116 right RIBA Library Photographs Collection, London; 117 Country Life Picture Library; 118 top Book Art & Architecture Picture Library/James Connell, Triad Architects; 118 bottom and 119 Book Art & Architecture Picture Library/Dennis Sharp Architects, London; 120 top Book Art & Architecture Picture Library; 120 bottom Country Life Picture Library; 121, 122 RIBA Library Photographs Collection, London; 123 Country Life Picture Library; 124 top RIBA Library Photographs Collection, London; 124 bottom, 125 Country Life Picture Library; 126 Country Life Picture Library/June Buck; 127, 128 Country Life Picture Library; 129 top RIBA Library Photographs Collection; 129 bottom, 130 Country Life Picture Library; 131 RIBA Library Photographs Collection; 132, 133, 134 top and bottom, 135 Country Life Picture Library; 136 Corbis UK Ltd/Historical Picture Archive/Philip de Bay; 137 left Collection Kharbine-Tapabor; 138-139, 140 left © 2002 Michael Freeman; 140 right, 141 top Kobal Collection/MGM; 141 bottom Corbis UK Ltd/Joseph Sohm, Chromosohm Inc; 142 © 2002 Michael Freeman; 143 Julius Shulman; 144, 145 © 2002 Michael Freeman; 146 top and bottom, 147, 148 and 149 Ernest Cormier Archive, Collection Centre Canadien d'Architecture/Canadian Centre for Architecture, Montréal; 150, 151 top © 2002 Michael Freeman; 151 bottom Kobal Collection/MGM; 152, 153 © 2002 Michael Freeman; 154 Archipress/Franck Eustache; 155 top Archipress/Lucien Hervé; 155 bottom, 156, 157 Fond d'archives conservé au Cabinet des dessins du Musée des Arts décoratifs, Paris; all rights reserved/Photos Zuber, Jean Colas; 158, 159 top English Heritage/ Jonathan Bailey; 159 bottom English Heritage Photo Library/Cozens Collection; 160-161, 162 top and bottom, 163 English Heritage/Jonathan Bailey; 164 top RIBA Library Photographs Collection, London; 164 bottom National Trust Photographic Library; 165, 166 National Trust Photographic Library/Philip Harris; 167 National Trust Photographic Library/Dennis Gilbert; 168 Science & Society Picture Library, Science Museum/National Railway Museum; 169 top Christie's Images 169 bottom © Archives Association French Lines – Le Havre.

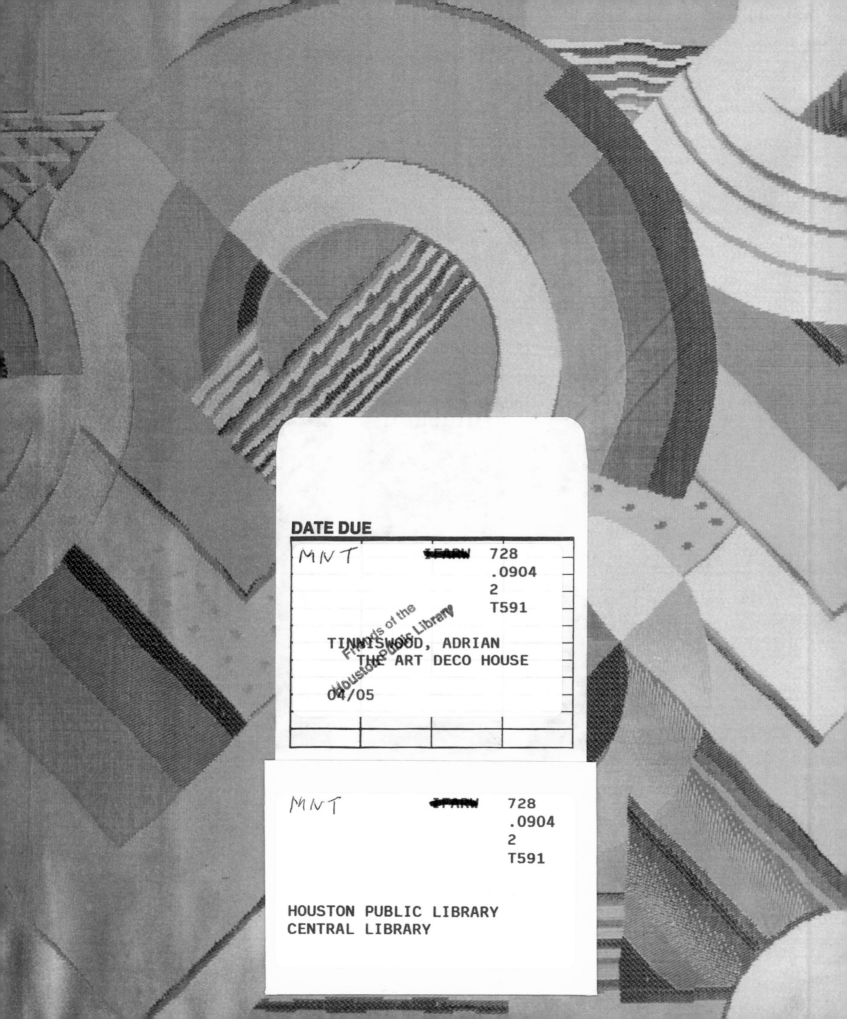